Summer and Sunny

AMIGURUMI DRESS-UP DOLLS
WITH BEACH PARTY PLAYSET

Summer and Sunny

AMIGURUMI DRESS-UP DOLLS WITH BEACH PARTY PLAYSET

CROCHET PATTERNS FOR 12" DOLLS plus DOLL CLOTHES, BEACH PLAYMAT & ACCESSORIES

Linda Wright

In memory of many days of beach play in my hometown, Santa Barbara

Also by Linda Wright

Chef Charlotte Amigurumi Dress-Up Doll with Tea Party Play Set
Honey Pie Amigurumi Dress-Up Doll with Picnic Play Set
Honey Bunny Amigurumi Dress Up-Doll with Garden Play Mat
Amigurumi Christmas Ornaments
Amigurumi Golf Club Covers
Amigurumi Animal Hats
Amigurumi Animal Hats Growing Up
Amigurumi Holiday Hats for 18-Inch Dolls
Amigurumi Animal Hats for 18-Inch Dolls
Amigurumi Toilet Paper Covers
Toilet Paper Origami On a Roll
Toilet Paper Origami

Credits
Photography: Linda and Randy Wright

All rights reserved. Permission is granted to copy or reprint portions for any noncommercial use, except they may not be posted online without permission. You may sell the finished products that you make yourself at your local bazaar, craft fair, etc. but not on the internet. Items cannot be mass produced without the publisher's written permission. Contact the publisher with licensing inquiries.

Copyright © 2023 Linda Wright
Edition 1.0

Lindaloo Enterprises
P.O. Box 90135
Santa Barbara, California 93190
United States
sales@lindaloo.com

ISBN: 978-1-937564-17-9
Library of Congress Control Number: 2023908367

CONTENTS

GETTING STARTED

Introduction — 8
Supplies — 10
Abbreviations — 13
Gauge — 13
How to Read a Pattern — 13

DOLLS

Summer and Sunny — 14

WARDROBE

Flamingo Swimsuit — 24
Anchor Swim Trunks — 26
2-piece Swimsuit — 27
Boardshorts — 28
Beach Wrap — 29
Beach Cover-Up — 30
Over-the-Rainbow Sundress — 32
Under-the Sea Sundress — 34
Striped Sundress — 36
Starfish Sundress — 38
Basic Shirt — 39
Crab Shirt — 40
Sunshine Shirt — 40
Palm Tree Shirt — 41
Sailboat Shirt — 42
Dolphin Shirt — 43
V-Neck Shirt — 44
Halter Top — 45
Polo Shirt — 46
Button-Front Shirt — 47
Shorts — 48
Jeans Shorts — 49
Jeans Skirt — 49
Shortalls — 50
Beach Pants — 51
Pajamas — 52
Underwear — 53
Cap — 54
Sun Hat — 55
Sandals — 56
Beach Clogs — 56
Sneakers — 57
Snug Boots — 57

BEACH PARTY

Beach Play Mat — 58

Accessories
Swim Ring	60
Beach Towel	61
Raft	62
Bodyboard	63
Beach Bucket	64
Sand Shovel	65
Rainbow Beach Ball	66
Mini FrizzBee	67
Sunscreen Lotion	67
Clams	68
Sand Dollars	69
Sand Castle	70
Beach Bag	72

Snacks
Peanut Butter & Jelly Sandwich	73
Bottled Water	74
Tortilla Chips	75
Ice Cream Cone	76
Orange Slice	77
Paper Plate	77

Friends
Ray the Stingray	78
Clawde the Crab	79
Seabert the Seagull	80
Starla the Starfish	82
Sandy the Dog	84

BED

Tropical Fish Sleeping Bag — 86

BASICS
Stitches	88
Techniques	90
Resources	93
Yarn	93

EXTRAS

Beach Party Invitations — 97

Summer and Sunny Coloring Page — 99

INTRODUCTION

Meet **Summer and Sunny** — a delightful duo that is crazy about the beach! They love floating in the ocean, building sand castles, tossing a beach ball, flinging a frizzbee, collecting clams, digging for sand dollars, and playing with their ocean friends. Sandy, the dog, jumps at the chance to go to the beach, too!

This book is brimming with colorful amigurumi and crochet patterns for a complete Beach Party. You will make 12" Summer and Sunny dolls, doll clothes, beach toys, snacks and a playmat. You will also find patterns for Starla the Starfish, Clawde the Crab, Ray the Stingray and Seabert the Seagull. The 24" x 40" Beach Playmat is sized to comfortably accommodate the dolls and their accessories for play, but if you want to make a bigger size, the formula is provided. For bedtime, a fish-shaped sleeping bag will keep each doll cozy!

Making doll clothes is a perfect way to unleash your creativity with different color combinations. Some of Summer's sweet sundresses feature ocean motifs. Her fringed halter is unique and chic. Most of the shirts are derived from the same basic pattern and you will learn various ways to embellish them using appliques, buttons, stripes or a collar. When dressing your dolls, remember that the clothes are designed to slide on feet-first.

You will find lots of stripes in this pattern collection. Stripes are beachy, bold and an easy way to elevate simple styles. Self-striping yarn is introduced for some designs. In that case, just crochet without changing colors and watch the stripes appear like magic! Of course, any striped item can be made without color changes for a different look.

Before starting, be sure to read the next 2 introductory pages plus the Stitches and Techniques sections at the back of the book for helpful tips. If you're new to crochet and like to learn by watching, excellent crocheting tutorials are offered at YouTube.com. I have assembled a collection of my favorite videos on Pinterest. You can see them at www.pinterest.com/LindalooEnt/ on a board named "Amigurumi Tutorials".

Amigurumi is a type of crochet for making 3D toys and objects — primarily with the single crochet stitch. Many amigurumi patterns are worked in the round. There are 2 ways to start a project in the round: the Magic Ring and the Chain 2 Method. I use the Magic Ring because once you learn it, you love it and never want to go back! However, the Chain 2 Method is definitely more beginner-friendly. My patterns typically use the Magic Ring, but you can absolutely replace this with the simple Chain 2 Method. To read more about this, see page 90.

Summer and Sunny are soft dolls with legs that rotate for sitting. Their arms are unstuffed and flexible. If you want to make a rigid doll that can hold a pose, wire can be added inside the arms, legs or both. (See "Adding Wire" on page 92.)

I strive to write my patterns with easy techniques and clear instructions so they will be fun and rewarding for crocheters of any level. Here are a few things I especially hope you enjoy:

- my first boy doll
- 2 cute hairstyles
- an adorable wardrobe
- the magic of self-striping yarn
- whimsical fish-shaped sleeping bags
- the rhythm of the ripple stitch (Beach Play Mat)
- reliving the enchantment of childhood as you crochet

This book uses U.S. crochet terms. If an instruction says sc, that is a U.S. single crochet — or a U.K. double crochet. Please refer to the stitch diagrams at the back of the book to be sure you are making the stitches as intended.

Summer and Sunny were inspired by my son and my best friend's daughter who grew up together as loyal friends. Living in a coastal community, their childhood included countless days of play at the beach. These dolls are companions for my previous dress-up dolls, **Honey Bunny**, **Honey Pie** and **Chef Charlotte**. All of the dolls are similar enough in size to be perfect playmates. They can share accessories from their playsets and many of their clothes. (*Honey Bunny* has shorter legs, so some adjustments will have to be made.)

I have included two little extras at the end of the book. The first is a set of invitations for your beach party. The second is a coloring page that is fun for all ages.

I hope this book sparks hours of happy crochet and imaginative play. If you enjoy my book, I would appreciate it so much if you leave a review at your online place of purchase. Other customers would appreciate it too!

So, gather up your yarn — and let's dive in!

♥ Linda

Supplies

Yarn

These projects have been made with acrylic yarns that are readily available and inexpensive. Worsted-weight yarn (#4) is used for items that need a sturdy structure. DK/Light Worsted (#3) is used for items that have a more delicate nature or that need to drape such as doll clothes. My go-to #3 yarn is Stylecraft "Special DK" from lovecrafts.com. It comes in a fantastic range of colors at a reasonable price. Be sure to check each pattern carefully for its yarn weight specification. The specific yarns I used are listed on pages 93-95.

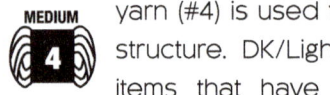

Crochet Hooks

The following hooks are used: E4/3.5mm, F5/3.75mm, G6/4mm and H8/5mm.

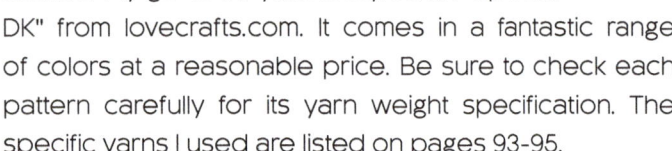

My favorite hook is the Clover Soft Touch. I love the thick handle and the shape of the head which inserts easily into a stitch.

Ruler

For measuring and marking.

Yarn Needles

You will need a large-eyed needle to sew the various pieces of your items together and also to finish them off by weaving the loose ends into your work. Yarn needles with a blunt point are readily available, but I frequently like to use one with a sharp point. These can be hard to find in stores, so if you'd like one, plan to shop online. My favorite is the Size 14 Chenille or Embroidery needle.

Stitch Markers

Stitch markers are used to keep track of where a round or row of crochet begins and ends. You can use a bobby pin, safety pin or purchased stitch markers. You can also use a scrap of yarn (see page 91). Making the correct number of stitches is important, so count to double check if ever you're not sure.

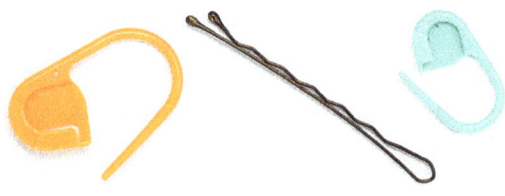

Scissors

You will need a small pair of sharp scissors.

Safety Eyes

Plastic safety eyes give amigurumi a professional look. Each eye has a post section and a washer. To attach with washer, work post into a gap between stitches, place washer against post, lay eye against a hard surface and press washer firmly. Eyes can also be attached with glue, omitting the washer.

Plastic safety eyes contain small parts. If the doll is for a child under age 3, I recommend using embroidery or small felt circles as alternatives.

Sewing Needle & Thread

If you don't have a supply of thread, one spool of clear nylon thread, called "invisible thread", will match everything. Besides sewing buttons or hook and eye closures in place, sewing thread can be used to sew crocheted pieces together.

Straight Pins

Use ball head dressmaker's pins or long corsage pins to hold pieces in place before sewing.

Row Counter

Well worth the investment, a row counter keeps track of what round or row of the pattern you are crocheting. A pencil and paper can also be used. Crochet apps for mobile devices are available too. A simple Android app that I like is called Minimalist Stitch Counter.

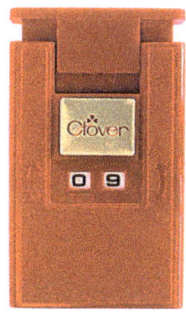

Removable Notes

Use small sticky notes to keep track of your place in a pattern. Every time you complete a round or a row, move the note down to reveal the next line of instructions. I wouldn't work without one!

Stuffing & Stuffing Tools

Polyester fiberfill, or polyfill, is the best stuffing material. Yarn scraps can be used for stuffing very small pieces. The eraser end of a new pencil, a blunt-tipped chopstick or tweezers make great stuffing tools. I highly recommend a pair of 6-inch straight-tip serrated tweezers. I find them invaluable for inserting stuffing through small openings.

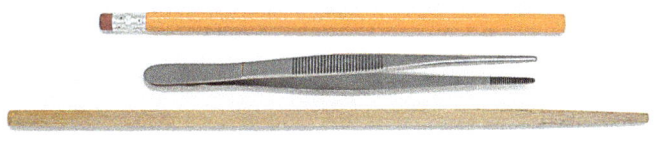

Glue

Glue is used for some of the assembly. Be sure to choose glues that dry clear. **Fast Grab Tacky Glue** and **Gem-Tac** are great for attaching plastic embellishments such as eyes and beads. **Fabri-Tac** is wonderful for joining fabric to fabric. **Tacky Glue, Elmer's Glue-All** and **Hot Glue** are good all-purpose choices. With any glue, I recommend practicing with scraps before working on your actual project to become familiar with how the glue reacts.

Beads

Beads elevate the look of amigurumi and bring an element of bling. I buy them at craft stores, Amazon and Etsy.

Bamboo Skewers

Thin bamboo skewers provide a great way to align stuffed pieces and hold them in position for sewing. Just push them right thru your fabric and stuffing. I used this method when assembling the Sand Castle, Sandy the Dog and Clawde the Crab.

Abbreviations

The following abbreviations are used:

yd = yard
st = stitch
ch = chain
sc = single crochet
hdc = half double crochet
dc = double crochet
sl st = slip stitch
rnd = round
sp = space
yo = yarn over
sc2tog = single crochet 2 stitches together
sc3tog = single crochet 3 stitches together
dc2tog = double crochet 2 stitches together
* * = a set of stitches
( ) = stitch count; also indicates a group of sts worked together in the same stitch or space

Terms

Right Side: The front side of crocheted fabric; the side that is usually seen or displayed.

Wrong Side: The back side of crocheted fabric; the side that is usually not seen and hidden.

Gauge

Gauge is a measure of how big your stitches are. It's very common for gauge to vary from person-to-person because not all crocheters stitch the same way. Yarn selection also affects gauge. Some yarns are thinner than others despite being in the same weight category.

Gauge is not critical in these projects. The main thing is to have the doll clothes fit your doll. Have fittings before the garments are done and make adjustments if needed.

To alter your gauge, adjust your crochet tension (tightness); change to a larger or smaller crochet hook; try a different brand of hook; or, try a different brand of yarn.

The following gauge is used in these patterns.

With **G6/4mm hook** and **DK, Light Worsted yarn**:
21 sc = 4"; 23 rows = 4"

With **G6/4mm hook** and **Worsted Weight yarn**:
19 sc = 4"; 22 rows = 4"

How to Read a Pattern

Each round or row is written on a new line. Most rounds have a repeated section of instructions that are written between two asterisks *like this*. The instruction between the asterisks is to be repeated as many times as indicated before you move on to the next step. At the end of a round, the total number of stitches to be made in that round is indicated in parentheses (like this).

Let's look at a round.

Rnd 6: *sc in next 4 sts, 2 sc in next st* 6 times (36 sts).

This means:

Rnd 6	This is the 6th round of the pattern.
sc in next 4 sts	Make 1 single crochet stitch in each of the next 4 stitches
2 sc in next st	Make 2 single crochet stitches, both in the same stitch
6 times	Repeat everything between * and * 6 times.
(36 sts)	The round will have a total of 36 stitches.

So, following the instructions for Round 6, you will:

single crochet in the next 4 sts, 2 sc in the next st,
single crochet in the next 4 sts, 2 sc in the next st,
single crochet in the next 4 sts, 2 sc in the next st,
single crochet in the next 4 sts, 2 sc in the next st,
single crochet in the next 4 sts, 2 sc in the next st,
single crochet in the next 4 sts, 2 sc in the next st,

for a total of 36 stitches.

Summer and Sunny

Summer and Sunny are made from worsted-weight yarn. These dolls were made with beige skin and blonde hair, but the skintone and hair can be customized in any way you wish. Use the same brand of yarn for the dolls and their wigs for the best fit. See page 93 for the specific yarns used here.

The doll parts are crocheted as continuous spirals by working in the round. When crocheting small cylinders such as the arms and legs, a running stitch marker is ideal (see page 91). The eraser end of a new pencil makes a great stuffing tool: by twisting the pencil as you push, the eraser will grab the stuffing.

The dolls' legs are attached by yarn jointing. This is an easy way to make movable legs. If you would like your doll to be able to hold a pose, wire can be added inside the arms and legs. Instructions for this are provided in the Techniques section on page 92. I wired my dolls in order to pose them for the photos in this book. Without wire, Summer and Sunny will be soft and cuddly with rotating legs that allow them to sit nicely.

SIZE

12" tall

SUPPLIES

G6/4mm crochet hook

110 yds of Worsted weight yarn in beige (per doll)

60 yds of Worsted weight yarn in lemon (Summer's hair)

50 yds of Worsted weight yarn in mustard (Sunny's hair)

2 black safety eyes, 10mm (per doll)

Glue (for eyes & fabric, see page 11)

Ball head sewing pins

Polyester fiberfill stuffing

Wood dowel, 3/16" diameter (optional neck support)

HEAD

Make a magic ring, ch 1.

Rnd 1: 6 sc in ring, pull ring closed tight (6 sts).

Rnd 2: 2 sc in each st around. Place marker for beginning of rnd and move marker up as each rnd is completed (12 sts).

Rnd 3: *sc in next st, 2 sc in next st* 6 times (18 sts).

Rnd 4: *sc in next 2 sts, 2 sc in next st* 6 times (24 sts).

Rnd 5: *sc in next 3 sts, 2 sc in next st* 6 times (30 sts).

Rnd 6: *sc in next 4 sts, 2 sc in next st* 6 times (36 sts).

Rnd 7: sc in each st around.

Rnd 8: *sc in next 5 sts, 2 sc in next st* 6 times (42 sts).

Rnds 9-13: sc in each st around.

Note: In Rnds 14-18, sc2tog can be used instead of invdec (see page 89).

Rnd 14: *sc in next 5 sts, invdec* 6 times (36 sts).

Rnd 15: *sc in next 4 sts, invdec* 6 times (30 sts).

Rnd 16: *sc in next 3 sts, invdec* 6 times (24 sts).

Rnd 17: *sc in next 2 sts, invdec* 6 times (18 sts).

Rnd 18: *sc in next st, invdec* 6 times (12 sts).

Sl st in next st. Fasten off.

BODY

Make a magic ring, ch 1.

Rnd 1: 8 sc in ring, pull ring closed tight (8 sts).

Rnd 2: *sc in next st, 2 sc in next st* 4 times. Place marker for beginning of rnd and move marker up as each rnd is completed (12 sts).

Rnd 3: *sc in next st, 2 sc in next st* 6 times (18 sts).

Rnd 4: *sc in next 2 sts, 2 sc in next st* 6 times (24 sts).

Rnds 5-17: sc in each st around.

Rnd 18: *sc in next 2 sts, sc2tog* 6 times (18 sts).

Rnd 19: *sc in next st, sc2tog* 6 times (12 sts).

Sl st in next st. Fasten off.

LEGS (MAKE 2)

Make a magic ring, ch 1.

Rnd 1: 6 sc in ring, pull ring closed tight (6 sts).

Rnd 2: *sc in next st, 2 sc in next st* 3 times. Place marker for beginning of rnd and move marker up as each rnd is completed (9 sts).

Rnds 3-23: sc in each st around.

Rnd 24: for **foot**, 2 sc in next st, 4 sc in next 2 sts, 2 sc in next st, sc in next 6 sts (18 sts).

Rnds 25-26: sc in each st around.

Rnd 27: sc2tog 9 times (9 sts).
Fasten off.

ARMS (MAKE 2)

Make a magic ring, ch 1.

Rnd 1: 9 sc in ring, pull ring closed tight (9 sts).

Rnds 2-3: sc in each st around. Place marker for beginning of rnd and move marker up as each rnd is completed.

Rnd 4: sc2tog twice, sc in next 5 sts (7 sts).

Rnds 5-22: sc in each st around.

Sl st in next st. Fasten off.

ASSEMBLY

Head: Stuff head firmly pushing stuffing outward against surface of sphere to fill out the space. **Stuff until circumference of head is 10" at the widest point so the wig fits.**

Body: Stuff body firmly. Sew head and body together, packing in more stuffing at the neck area for support when seam is nearly closed. Optional: For extra support, insert a 4" piece of dowel in the neck area as you stuff.

Legs: Stuff the legs. To close hole, thread ending tail onto needle, weave needle in and out around post of each st and pull tight. Hide yarn tails inside legs.

The legs are attached by yarn-jointing. Mark position for legs on each side of body in groove between Rnds 5-6 using a pin or stitch marker (see locations A and B in Fig. X).

Lay body and legs as shown in Fig. X. I used bobby pins to keep the feet facing forward. Cut a generous length of yarn and thread it on a blunt-tipped yarn needle.

1. Push needle into body at A and out at B leaving a tail.

2. Push needle into first leg at C (groove between Rnds 2-3) and out at D.

3. Straddle 2 sts at D, sew back into leg and out in exact same st at C. Be sure the st at D is centered on outer leg so your leg hangs straight.

4. Push needle back in at B and out at A going into exact same sts as before.

5. Push needle into second leg at E (groove between Rnds 2-3) and out at F.

6. Straddle 2 sts at F, sew back into leg and out in exact same st at E. Be sure the st at F is centered on outer leg so your leg hangs straight.

Pull yarn to tighten legs, pulling them into the body a bit. Make sure legs are pulled tight. They will loosen up slightly with time. For extra strength, repeat these steps. Knot yarn ends together and hide tails inside body.

Arms: With eraser end of new pencil, push stuffing into hand only; do not stuff arm. Sew an arm to each side, 1 rnd down from top of body (see photos on page 14).

Glue **eyes** between Rnds 12-13 with an interspace of 8-9 sts; or mark the locations now, but do the final gluing after the hair is done to be sure you like the look.

Embroider **nose** 2 rows below eyes.

Weave in ends. ♥

Figure X

Legs are Done

SUMMER'S HAIR

Notes:

• For Summer's wig, sometimes you will be instructed to work into the Right Side of the Wig Base, and sometimes into the Wrong Side. You will see close-up photos to show the Right and Wrong sides of the piece. Also, when looking at the Wig Base, the stitches that faced you as you crocheted Rnds 1-2 are the Right Side..

• A chain 1 at the beginning of a row is for turning your work and does not count as a stitch.

WIG BASE

Make a magic ring, ch 1.

Rnd 1: 7 sc in ring, pull ring closed tight (7 sts).

Rnd 2: 2 sc in each st around (14 sts).

Now work in rows.

Row 3: ch 1, turn, working in **front loops only**, *sc in next 2 sts, 2 sc in next st* 3 times (12 sts).

Row 4: ch 1, turn, resuming work in **both loops**, *sc in next 3 sts, 2 sc in next st* 3 times (15 sts).

Row 5: ch 1, turn, *sc in next 4 sts, 2 sc in next st* 3 times (18 sts).

Row 6: ch 1, turn, *sc in next 5 sts, 2 sc in next st* 3 times (21 sts).

Rows 7-10: ch 1, turn, **dc** in each st across (21 sts).

Fasten off.

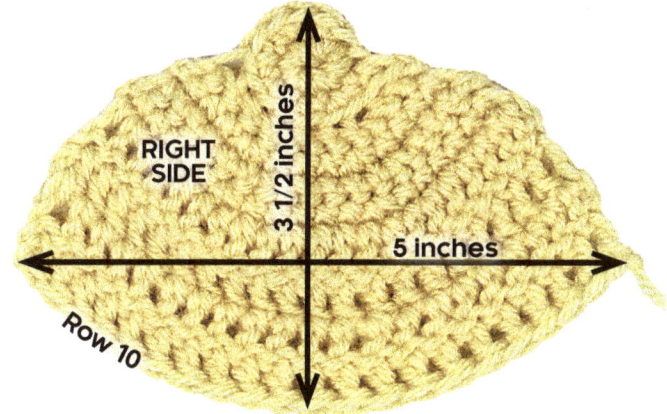

LOWER BANGS

Six strands of Lower Bangs are made in Rnd 2 of Wig Base.

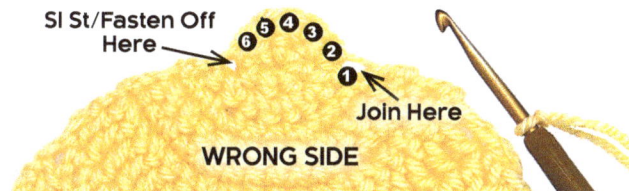

With **wrong side** facing you, join with sl st in gap labeled ❶ in photo above.

Row 1: ch 11, turn, sl st in 2nd ch from hook, sc in next ch, hdc in next ch, dc in next 7 chs (10 sts). **See Row 1 of Sunny's Bangs, page 20, for photos of this step.**

Rows 2-5: sl st in **back loop of** next st, ch 10, turn, sl st in 2nd ch from hook, sc in next ch, hdc in next ch, dc in next 6 chs (9 sts).

Row 6: sl st in **back loop of** next st, ch 11, turn, sl st in 2nd ch from hook, sc in next ch, hdc in next ch, dc in next 7 chs (10 sts). Sl st in next st. Fasten off.

See completed Lower Bangs in pic below. Notice how bangs curve. Wig will be placed with curves hugging doll's head.

UPPER BANGS

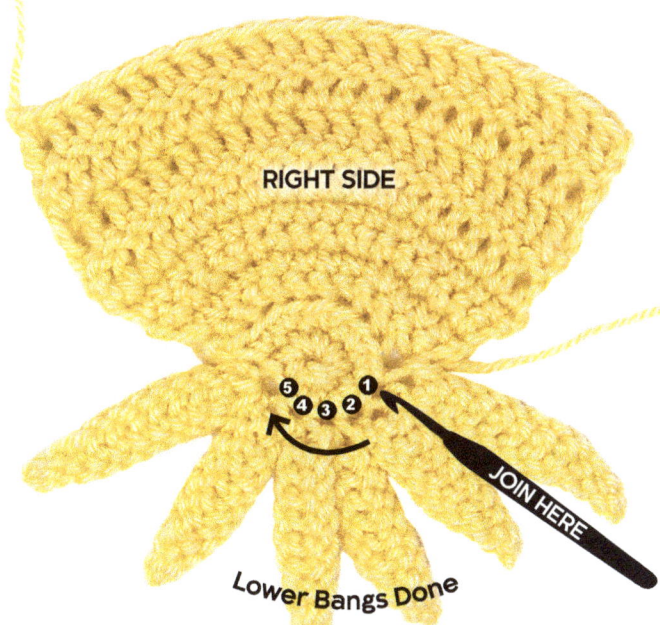

Flip Wig Base so **right side** faces you. Upper Bangs are made in 5 unworked loops marked in photo above.

Join with sl st at ❶ with hook positioned as pictured.

Row 1: ch 12, turn, sl st in 2nd ch from hook, sc in next ch, hdc in next ch, dc in next 8 chs (11 sts).

Rows 2-5: sl st in next st, ch 12, turn, sl st in 2nd ch from hook, sc in next ch, hdc in next ch, dc in next 8 chs (11 sts). Sl st in next st. Fasten off.

Next, each Back Panel is made with 6 connected rows.

BACK PANEL A

Row 1: ch 9, turn, sl st in 2nd ch from hook, sc in next ch, hdc in next ch, dc in next 5 chs (8 sts).

Rows 2-3: ch 12, turn, sl st in 2nd ch from hook, sc in next ch, hdc in next ch, dc in next 8 chs (11 sts).

Row 4: ch 14, turn, sl st in 2nd ch from hook, sc in next ch, hdc in next ch, dc in next 10 chs (13 sts).

Rows 5-6: ch 16, turn, sl st in 2nd ch from hook, sc in next ch, hdc in next ch, dc in next 12 chs (15 sts).

Fasten off.

BACK PANEL B

Rows 1-2: ch 16, turn, sl st in 2nd ch from hook, sc in next ch, hdc in next ch, dc in next 12 chs (15 sts).

Row 3: ch 14, turn, sl st in 2nd ch from hook, sc in next ch, hdc in next ch, dc in next 10 chs (13 sts).

Rows 4-5: ch 12, turn, sl st in 2nd ch from hook, sc in next ch, hdc in next ch, dc in next 8 chs (11 sts).

Row 6: ch 9, turn, sl st in 2nd ch from hook, sc in next ch, hdc in next ch, dc in next 5 chs (8 sts).

Fasten off.

PIGTAIL PIECES (MAKE 6)

Each Pigtail Piece is made from 2 connected rows. These are bundled to create Summer's pigtails.

Leave a 12" starting tail.

Rows 1-2: ch 8, turn, sl st in 2nd ch from hook and in each remaining ch across (7 sts).

Fasten off with 12" tail.

For each pigtail, stack 3 Pigtail Pieces as shown in Fig. A. Tie tails X and Y together in a half knot (1 time around) to look like Fig. B.

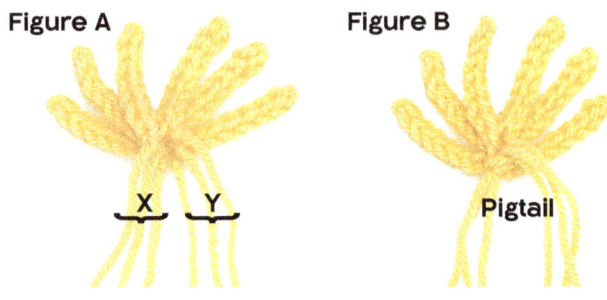

TOPPER

Ch 2.

Row 1: 3 sc in 2nd ch from hook (3 sts).

Row 2: ch 1, turn, 2 sc in each st across (6 sts).

Fasten off. Trim tails to 1/2 inch.

TOPPER STRANDS (MAKE 3)

Row 1: ch 14, turn, sl st in 2nd ch from hook and in each remaining ch across (13 sts). Fasten off.

FINISHING

1. Position and pin Wig Base on head. Align at top by inserting a ball-head pin thru center of Rnd 1 of Wig Base then into center of Rnd 1 of head.

2. Sew Wig Base in place avoiding the bangs.

3. Locate left and right strands of Lower Bangs (Rows 1 and 6), butt them against Wig Base (see arrow) and glue in place with fabric glue.

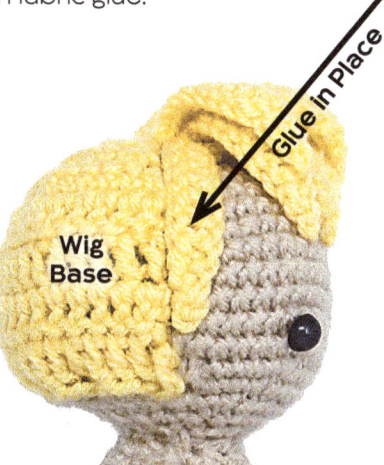

4. Pin Back Panel A against back of Wig Base. Curve of hair strands follows curve of head. Shortest hair strand is at bottom and extends slightly below edge of Wig Base at **X** in photo below. Note how hair strands leave a recess at **Y** in photo below for pigtail placement. Sew panel in place along center back, then lift hair strands one-by-one and glue in position with fabric glue. Replace pin until glue dries. (Be sure head of pin doesn't get glued to hair.)

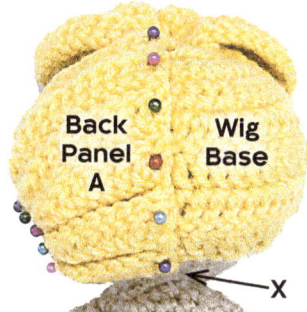

Repeat with Back Panel B on other side of head.

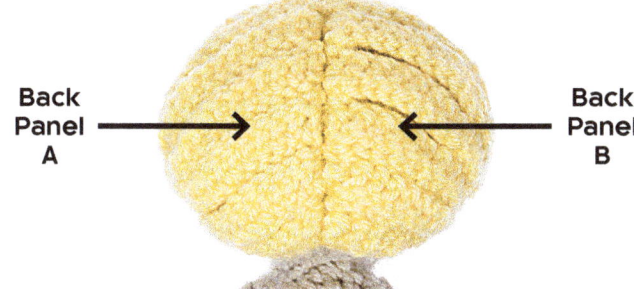

5. Pin remaining bangs in place. Working one-by-one, remove pin from bangs, apply fabric glue, lay back in position and replace pin until glue is dry. (Be sure head of pin doesn't get glued to hair.)

6. Glue Topper to indentation at top of Wig Base, wrong side up, tucking yarn tails underneath.

7. Thread yarn tails of pigtails into needle 1 or 2 strands at a time and sew a pigtail to each side of head at area **Y**. Hide yarn tails inside head.

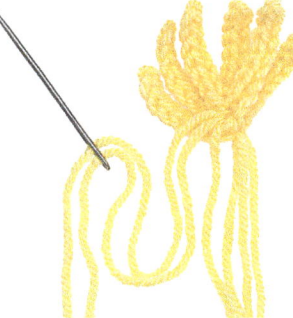

8. Sew Topper Strands thru Topper to hang equidistantly over bangs (see 3 dots below). Hide yarn tails inside head. Glue Topper Strands in place. ♥

SUNNY'S HAIR

Notes:

- For Sunny's wig, sometimes you will be instructed to work into the Right Side of the Wig Base, and sometimes into the Wrong Side. You will see close-up photos to show the Right and Wrong sides of the piece. Also, when looking at the Wig Base, the stitches that faced you as you crocheted Rnds 1-2 are the Right Side..

- A chain 1 at the beginning of a row is for turning your work and does not count as a stitch.

WIG BASE

Make a magic ring, ch 1.

Rnd 1: 7 sc in ring, pull ring closed tight (7 sts).

Rnd 2: 2 sc in each st around (14 sts).

Now work in rows.

Row 3: ch 1, turn, working in **front loops only**, *sc in next 2 sts, 2 sc in next st* 3 times (12 sts).

Row 4: ch 1, turn, resuming work in **both loops**, *sc in next 3 sts, 2 sc in next st* 3 times (15 sts).

Row 5: ch 1, turn, *sc in next 4 sts, 2 sc in next st* 3 times (18 sts).

Row 6: ch 1, turn, *sc in next 5 sts, 2 sc in next st* 3 times (21 sts).

Rows 7-9: ch 1, turn, **dc** in each st across (21 sts).

Fasten off.

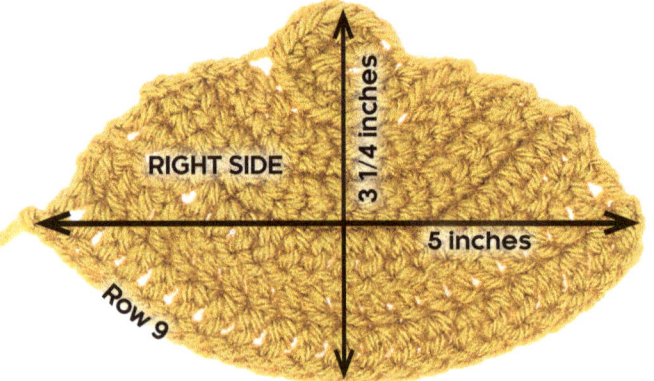

BANGS

Six strands of Bangs are made in Rnd 2 of Wig Base.

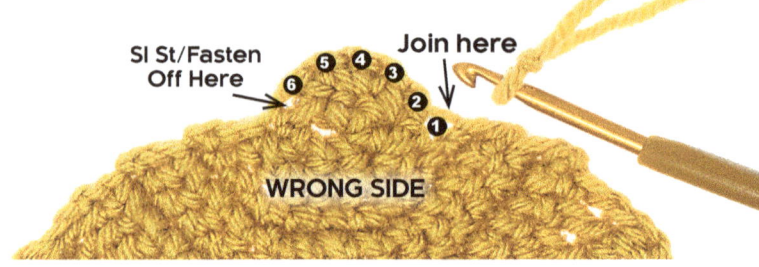

With **wrong side** of Wig Base facing you, join with sl st in gap labeled ❶ in photo above.

Row 1: ch 11, turn, sl st in 2nd ch from hook, sc in next ch, hdc in next ch, dc in next 7 chs (10 sts).

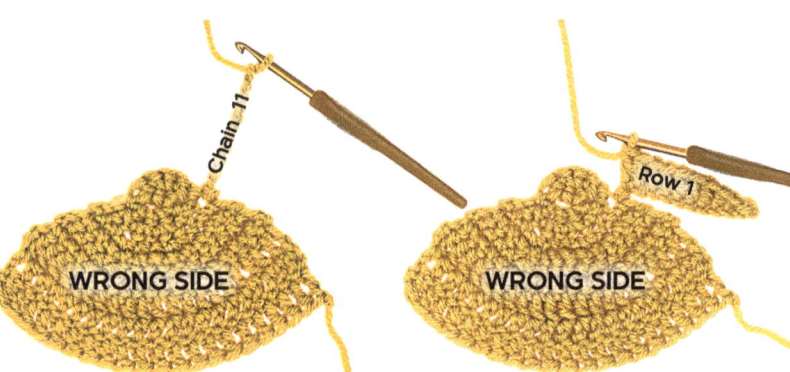

Rows 2-5: sl st in **back loop** of next st, ch 10, turn, sl st in 2nd ch from hook, sc in next ch, hdc in next ch, dc in next 6 chs (9 sts).

Row 6: sl st in **back loop** of next st, ch 11, turn, sl st in 2nd ch from hook, sc in next ch, hdc in next ch, dc in next 7 chs (10 sts). Sl st in next st. Fasten off.

Notice how the Bangs curve. Wig will be placed with curves hugging doll's head.

Bangs are Done

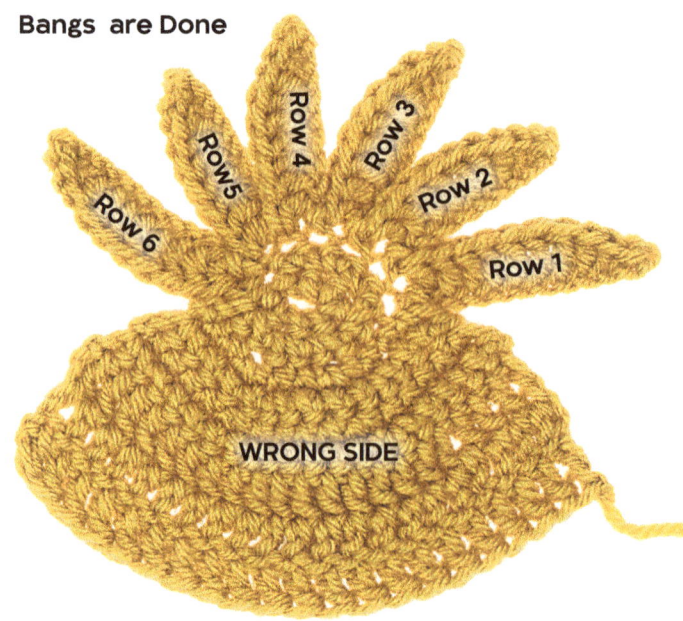

RING OF HAIR STRANDS

Flip Wig Base so **right side** faces you. Ring of Hair Strands is made in 14 unworked loops marked with dots in photo below.

NAPE HAIR STRANDS

Flip Wig Base as shown in photo below.

Join with sl st at dot.

Join with sl st at ❶ with hook positioned as shown.

Row 1: ch 12, sl st in 2nd ch from hook, sc in next ch, hdc in next ch, dc in next 8 chs (11 sts).

Rows 2-14: sl st in next st, ch 12, turn, sl st in 2nd ch from hook, sc in next ch, hdc in next ch, dc in next 8 chs (11 sts).

Sl st in next st. Fasten off.

Row 1: ch 7, turn, sl st in 2nd ch from hook, sc in next ch, hdc in next 4 chs (6 sts).

Rows 2-10: sl st in next 2 sts, ch 7, turn, sl st in 2nd ch from hook, sc in next ch, hdc in next 4 chs (6 sts).

Sl st in next 2 sts. Fasten off.

Top View of Wig after Ring-of-Hair-Strands is done.

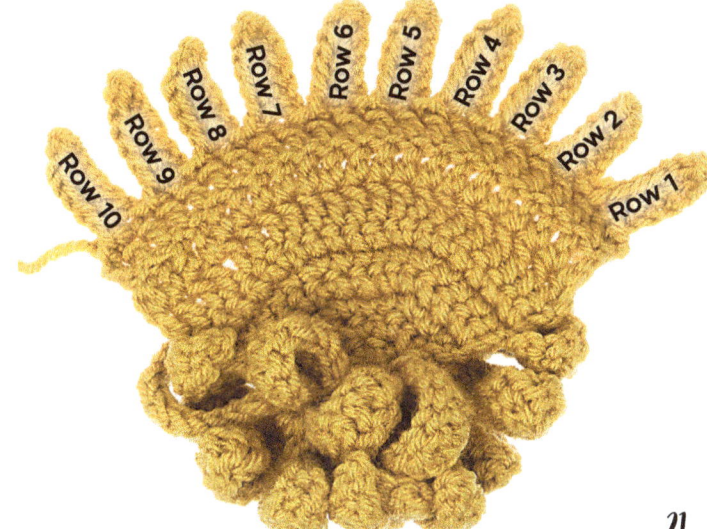

TOPPER

Make a magic ring, ch 1.

Rnd 1: 7 sc in ring, pull ring closed tight (7 sts).

Rnd 2: 2 sc in each st around (14 sts).

Sl st in next st. Fasten off. Trim tails to 1 inch.

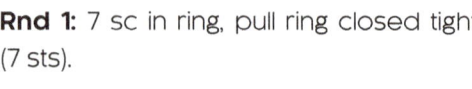

TOPPER STRANDS (MAKE 6)

Row 1: ch 14, turn, sl st in 2nd ch from hook and in each remaining ch across (13 sts). Fasten off.

FINISHING

1. Position and pin Wig Base on head. Align at top by inserting a ball-head pin thru center of Rnd 1 of Wig Base then into center of Rnd 1 of head.

2. Sew Wig Base in place avoiding all loose hair strands at top and nape.

3. Locate left and right strands of Bangs (Rows 1 and 6), butt against Wig Base and glue in place with fabric glue. **See arrow in next photo.**

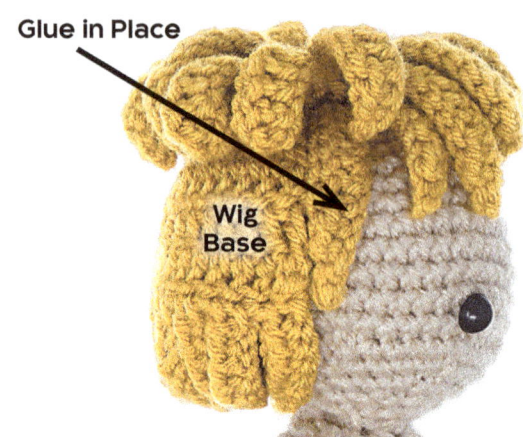

4. Pin remaining Bangs and Ring-of-Hair-Strands in position as pictured below. Working one-by-one, remove pin from hair strand, apply fabric glue, lay back in position and replace pin until glue dries. (Be sure head of pin doesn't get glued to hair.)

5. Glue Topper to indentation at top of Wig Base, wrong side up, tucking yarn tails underneath.

6. Sew Topper Strands thru Topper to hang equidistantly around wig. (See front 3 Topper Strands marked with dots in photo below). Hide yarn tails inside head. Glue strands in place.

7. Glue Nape Hair Strands against head, if desired. ♥

Flamingo Swimsuit

The swimsuit is worked back and forth in rows, starting at the bottom. After the panty section is created, a slit-back bodice is made.

SUPPLIES

G6/4mm and F5/3.75mm crochet hooks

Small amount of DK, Light Worsted yarn in red, pink, white & black

Black bead, 4mm

Button, 1/2" diameter

Sewing thread

Note: A chain 1 at the beginning of a row is for turning your work and does not count as a stitch.

PANTY

With red yarn and G6/4mm crochet hook, leave a 9" starting tail, ch 19.

Row 1: sc in 2nd ch from hook and in each remaining ch across (18 sts).

Row 2: ch 1, turn, sc in each st across.

Row 3: ch 1, turn, sc2tog, sc in next 14 sts, sc2tog (16 sts).

Row 4: ch 1, turn, sc2tog, sc in next 12 sts, sc2tog (14 sts).

Row 5: ch 1, turn, sc2tog, sc in next 10 sts, sc2tog (12 sts).

Row 6: ch 1, turn, sc2tog twice, sc in next 4 sts, sc2tog twice (8 sts).

Row 7: ch 1, turn, sc2tog 4 times (4 sts).

Row 8: ch 1, turn, sc2tog twice (2 sts).

Row 9: ch 1, turn, sc2tog (1 st).

Row 10: ch 1, turn, 2 sc in next st (2 sts).

Row 11: ch 1, turn, 2 sc in next 2 sts (4 sts).

Row 12: ch 1, turn, 2 sc in next 4 sts (8 sts).

Row 13: ch 1, turn, 2 sc in next 2 sts, sc in next 4 sts, 2 sc in next 2 sts (12 sts).

Row 14: ch 1, turn, 2 sc in next st, sc in next 10 sts, 2 sc in next st (14 sts).

Row 15: ch 1, turn, 2 sc in next st, sc in next 12 sts, 2 sc in next st (16 sts).

Row 16: ch 1, turn, 2 sc in next st, sc in next 14 sts, 2 sc in next st (18 sts).

Rows 17-18: ch 1, turn, sc in each st across.

Fasten off with 9" tail.

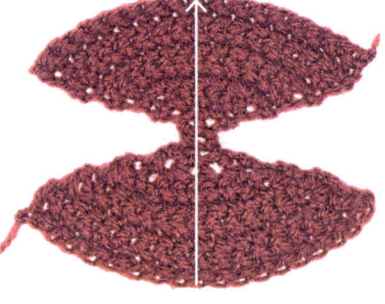

Fold panty in half at crotch. Using yarn tails, sew together at sides about 1/2", making sure leg openings can accommodate doll's legs (see dotted lines, Fig. A).

Figure A

BODICE

The bodice is worked back-and-forth in rows to create an opening at the back of the swimsuit.

With G6/4mm crochet hook, join with sc at center back of panty (see dot, Fig. B).

Figure B

Row 19: sc in each st across (36 sts).

Rows 20-24: ch 1, turn, sc in each st across.

Row 25: ch 1, turn, *sc in next 4 sts, sc2tog* 6 times (30 sts).

Row 26: ch 1, turn, *sc in next 3 sts, sc2tog* 6 times (24 sts).

Row 27: sc in each st across.

Row 28: ch 1, turn, sc in first 4 sts; for **armhole**, ch 10 loosely, skip next 4 sts; sc in next 8 sts; for **armhole**, ch 10 loosely, skip next 4 sts; sc in last 4 sts (16 sts, 20 ch).

Row 29: ch 1, turn, sc in each st or ch across (36 sts).

Row 30: ch 1, do not turn, sc around back opening until 1 st remains; for **button loop**, ch 3, sc in next st. Fasten off.

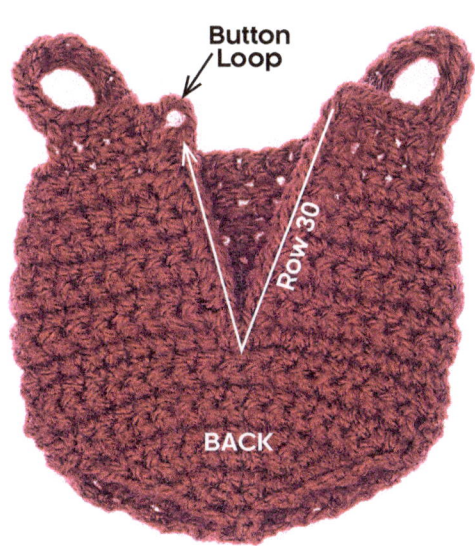

Sew button to corner opposite loop.

Leg Trim: Work a round of sc around leg openings, joining new yarn with sl st and ending with sl st.

Weave in ends.

FLAMINGO APPLIQUE

BODY

With pink yarn and F5/3.75mm crochet hook, make a magic ring, ch 1.

Rnd 1: 6 sc in ring, pull ring closed tight (6 sts).

Rnd 2: 2 sc in each st around (12 sts).

Rnd 3: *sc in next st, 2 sc in next st* 6 times (18 sts).

Sl st in next st. Fasten off.

HEAD & NECK

With pink yarn and F5/3.75mm crochet hook, make a magic ring, ch 1.

Rnd 1: for **head**, 10 sc in ring, pull ring closed tight (10 sts).

Row 2: for **neck**, sl st in next st, loosely ch 15.

Fasten off.

BEAK

The beak is made from a short chain. You will change colors for the final chain to create the beak's black tip.

Row 1: With white yarn and F5/3.75mm crochet hook, ch 3; release white yarn, yarn over with black yarn and pull thru loop on hook (4 chs).

Fasten off. Pull yarn tails gently to tighten the sts.

FINISHING

Arrange parts of flamingo applique on swimsuit as pictured. Tuck excess length of neck under body. Sew or glue in place. Tip: for **beak**, set it in place, sew yarn tails thru to inside of swimsuit and weave in ends.

Sew bead in place for eye. ♥

Anchors Away Swim Trunks

Fig. A

To form **legs**, sew first and last rows together on each side.

For **waistband**, join with sc at center back.

Rnds 13-14: sc in each st around.

Sl st in next st. Fasten off. Weave in ends.

ANCHOR APPLIQUE

VERTICAL SHANK

Ch 12. Fasten off.

To create **ring** at top of shank, sew upper tail down thru 5th st from where you fastened off.

CROSSBAR

Ch 6. Fasten off.

LOWER V

Ch 10. Fasten off.

Glue parts of anchor in place as shown in photo, sewing yarn tails thru to inside of garment. Knot ends together and trim excess.

FINISHING

Thread a yarn needle with elastic cord and weave thru back of stitches around **waistband**. Try shorts on doll to get the right tension and knot ends of elastic together. ♥

The easy swim trunks are made with dc in rows. This pattern can also be used for shorts. Elastic bead cord makes terrific waistband elastic.

SUPPLIES

G6/4mm crochet hook

Small amount of DK, Light Worsted yarn in gold and blue

Fabric glue

Stretch Magic clear elastic bead cord (.7mm)

SIDES (MAKE 2)

With gold yarn, ch 13 loosely.

Rows 1-12: ch 1, turn, dc in each st across (13 sts).

Fasten off.

Place pieces side-by-side. For **center front** seam, sew top 10 sts together. See dotted line in Fig. A.

Repeat for **center back** seam.

2-Piece Swimsuit

SUPPLIES

G6/4mm crochet hook

Small amount of DK, Light Worsted yarn in blue and pink

TOP

With blue yarn, ch 9.

Row 1: sc in 2nd ch from hook and in each remaining ch across (8 sts).

Row 2: ch 1, turn, 2 sc in 1st st, sc in next 6 sts, 2 sc in last st (10 sts).

Row 3: ch 1, turn, 2 sc in 1st st, sc in next 8 sts, 2 sc in last st (12 sts).

Row 4: ch 1, turn, 2 sc in 1st st, sc in next 10 sts, 2 sc in last st (14 sts).

Row 5: ch 1, turn, 2 sc in 1st st, sc in next 12 sts, 2 sc in last st (16 sts).

Row 6: ch 1, turn, 2 sc in 1st st, sc in next 14 sts, 2 sc in last st (18 sts).

Row 7: ch 1, turn, 2 sc in 1st st, sc in next 16 sts, 2 sc in last st (20 sts).

Row 8: ch 1, turn, 2 sc in 1st st, sc in next 18 sts, 2 sc in last st (22 sts). Fasten off. Weave in ends.

TIES

With pink yarn, ch 35, sc in next 8 sts across **Edge A**, ch 35 (8 sts, 70 chs). Fasten off, trim tails to 1/4 inch.

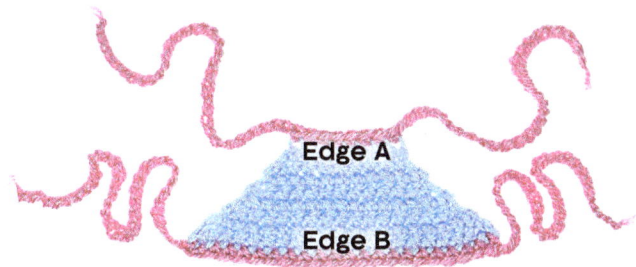

With pink yarn, ch 35, sc in next 22 sts across **Edge B**, ch 35 (22 sts, 70 chs). Fasten off, trim tails to 1/4 inch.

PANTY

With blue yarn, ch 13.

Row 1: sc in 2nd ch from hook and in each remaining ch across (12 sts).

Rows 2-3: ch 1, turn, sc in each st across.

Row 4: ch 1, turn, sc2tog, sc in next 8 sts, sc2tog (10 sts).

Row 5: ch 1, turn, sc2tog, sc in next 6 sts, sc2tog (8 sts).

Row 6: ch 1, turn, sc2tog, sc in next 4 sts, sc2tog (6 sts).

Row 7: ch 1, turn, sc2tog, sc in next 2 sts, sc2tog (4 sts).

Row 8: ch 1, turn, sc2tog twice (2 sts).

Row 9: ch 1, turn, sc2tog (1 st).

Row 10: ch 1, turn, 2 sc in next st (2 sts).

Row 11: ch 1, turn, 2 sc in next 2 sts (4 sts).

Row 12: ch 1, turn, 2 sc in next st, sc in next 2 sts, 2 sc in next st (6 sts).

Row 13: ch 1, turn, 2 sc in next st, sc in next 4 sts, 2 sc in next st (8 sts).

Row 14: ch 1, turn, 2 sc in next st, sc in next 6 sts, 2 sc in next st (10 sts).

Row 15: ch 1, turn, 2 sc in next st, sc in next 8 sts, 2 sc in next st (12 sts).

Rows 16-18: ch 1, turn, sc in each st across.

Do not fasten off. Fold panty in half at crotch. Next you will connect upper edges of panty while working in a round.

Rnd 19: sc in each st around; change to pink yarn in last st (24 sts).

Rnd 20: sc in each st around. Sl st in next st. Fasten off.

Leg trim: join blue yarn at leg openings, sc in each st around. Fasten off.

Weave in ends. ♥

Boardshorts

Rnd 6: for **1st leg**, ch 2 (counts as dc), dc in next 17 sts, skip next 18 sts, join with sl st in 1st dc (18 sts).

Rnds 7-9: ch 2 (counts as dc), dc in next 17 sts, join with sl st in 1st dc (18 sts).

Fasten off.

Rnd 10: for **second leg**, join turquoise yarn on Rnd 5, ch 2 (counts as dc), dc in next 17 sts, join with sl st in 1st dc (18 sts).

Rnds 11-13: ch 2 (counts as dc), dc in next 17 sts, join with sl st in 1st dc (18 sts).

Fasten off.

Sew opening at crotch closed. Weave in ends.

For **drawstring**, chain a string 16" long with turquoise yarn. Starting at center front, use blunt yarn needle to weave drawstring thru sts of Rnd 1. Trim tails of drawstring to 1/2". ♥

Boardshorts are loose-fitting shorts with a drawstring. Starting at the waist, these are crocheted in joined rounds of dc. You will see Sunny wearing Boardshorts in different color combinations on the front cover and elsewhere in the book.

SUPPLIES

G6/4mm crochet hook

Small amount of DK, Light Worsted yarn in coral, gray and turquoise

With coral yarn, ch 36, join with sl st in 1st ch to make a ring using care not to twist the chain.

Rnds 1-3: ch 2 (counts as dc), dc in each st around, sl st in 1st dc to join the rnd; change to gray yarn in last st of Rnd 3. Place marker for beginning of rnd and move marker up as each rnd is completed (36 sts).

Rnds 4-5: ch 2 (counts as dc), dc in each st around, sl st in 1st dc to join the rnd; change to turquoise yarn in last st of Rnd 5 (36 sts).

Beach Wrap

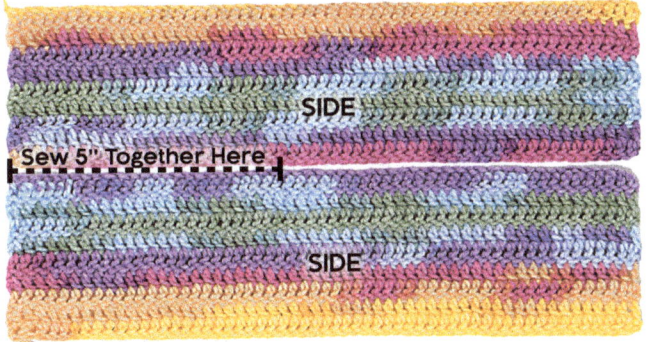

Figure A

Fold piece in half widthwise. Sew layers together 3" at each side to make armholes (see Fig. B).

Figure B

Weave in ends. ♥

The multi-color Beach Wrap was made with self-striping yarn. This type of yarn gradually changes color as you crochet. It's great fun to watch the stripes appear!

SUPPLIES

G6/4mm crochet hook

100 yds of DK, Light Worsted yarn, self-striping

Invisible sewing thread

Note: A chain 1 at the beginning of a row is for turning your work and does not count as a stitch.

SIDES (MAKE 2)

Ch 57.

Rows 1-9: ch 1, turn, dc in each st across (57 sts).

Fasten off.

Lay rectangles side-by-side. Sew 5" together with invisible sewing thread and whip stitch (see Fig. A).

Beach Cover-Up

The Beach Cover-Up has a generous hood that can even accommodate Summer's pigtails. Instructions are provided for this 4-color version, but the cover-up is also nice in one solid color made from 160 yards of yarn.

SUPPLIES

G6/4mm crochet hook

Small amount of DK, Light Worsted yarn in turquoise, navy, orange & yellow

Sewing thread in navy and invisible

4 hook and eye fasteners

Note: A chain 1 at the beginning of a row is for turning your work and does not count as a stitch.

FRONTS (MAKE 2)

With turquoise yarn, ch 25.

Rows 1-4: ch 1, turn, dc in each st across (25 sts).

Rows 5-6: ch 1, turn, dc in next 22 sts (22 sts)

Fasten off.

BACK

With turquoise yarn, ch 25.

Rows 1-4: ch 1, turn, dc in each st across (25 sts).

Rows 5-9: ch 1, turn, dc in next 22 sts (22 sts).

Row 10: ch 4, turn, dc in 2nd ch from hook and each remaining ch or st across (25 sts).

Rows 11-13: ch 1, turn, dc in each st across (25 sts).

Fasten off.

SLEEVES (MAKE 2)

Make 1 with orange yarn and 1 with yellow yarn.

Ch 12.

Rows 1-10: ch 1, turn, dc in each st across (12 sts).

Fasten off.

ASSEMBLY

With invisible thread, sew fronts, back and sleeves together as pictured in Fig. A.

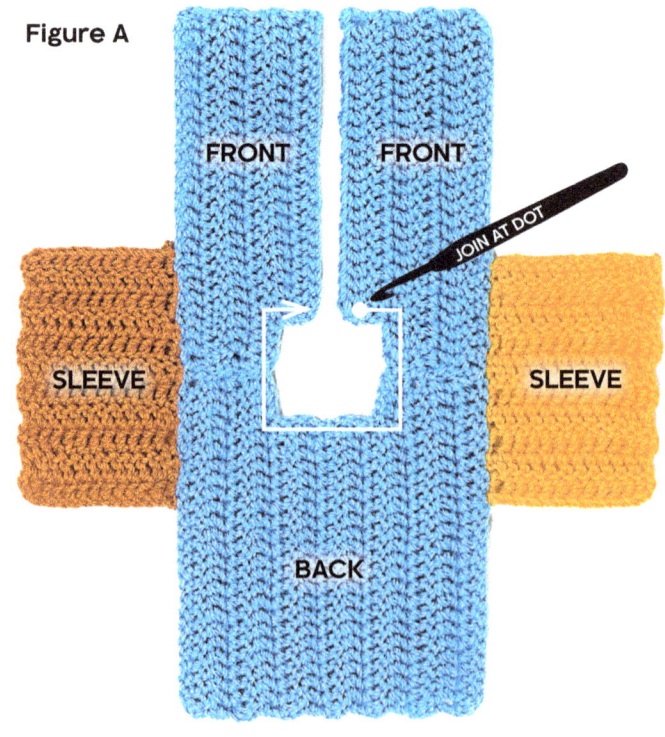

HOOD

Join navy yarn at dot in Fig. A.

Row 1: referring to arrow in Fig. A, dc in each st around neckline (30 sts).

Row 2: ch 1, turn, *dc in next 4 sts, 2 dc in next st* 6 times (36 sts).

Row 3: ch 1, turn, *dc in next 5 sts, 2 dc in next st* 6 times (42 sts).

Row 4: ch 1, turn, dc in each st across (42 sts).

Row 5: ch 1, turn, *dc in next 6 sts, 2 dc in next st* 6 times (48 sts).

Rows 6-11 ch 1, turn, dc in each st across (48 sts).

Row 12: ch 1, turn, dc in next 22 sts, dc2tog **twice**, dc in next 22 sts (46 sts).

Row 13: ch 1, turn, dc in next 21 sts, dc2tog **twice**, dc in next 21 sts (44 sts).

Row 14: ch 1, turn, dc in next 20 sts, dc2tog **twice**, dc in next 20 sts (42 sts).

Row 15: ch 1, turn, dc in next 19 sts, dc2tog **twice**, dc in next 19 sts (40 sts).

Row 16: ch 1, turn, dc in next 18 sts, dc2tog **twice**, dc in next 18 sts (38 sts).

Row 17: ch 1, turn, dc in next 17 sts, dc2tog **twice**, dc in next 17 sts (36 sts).

Row 18: ch 1, turn, dc in next 10 sts, dc2tog **8 times**, dc in next 10 sts (28 sts).

Fasten off with long tail.

Turn cover-up inside-out. Sew top of hood closed with whip stitch. See Fig. B.

EDGE TRIM

Looking at front of cover-up, join with sc at lower right corner, inserting your hook into wrong side of fabric.

Row 1: sc in each st around front, hood and remaining front.

Row 2: ch 1, turn, sc in each st around. Fasten off.

FINISHING

Weave in ends.

Sew hook & eye fasteners at 1 1/2" intervals along back side of front edges. ♥

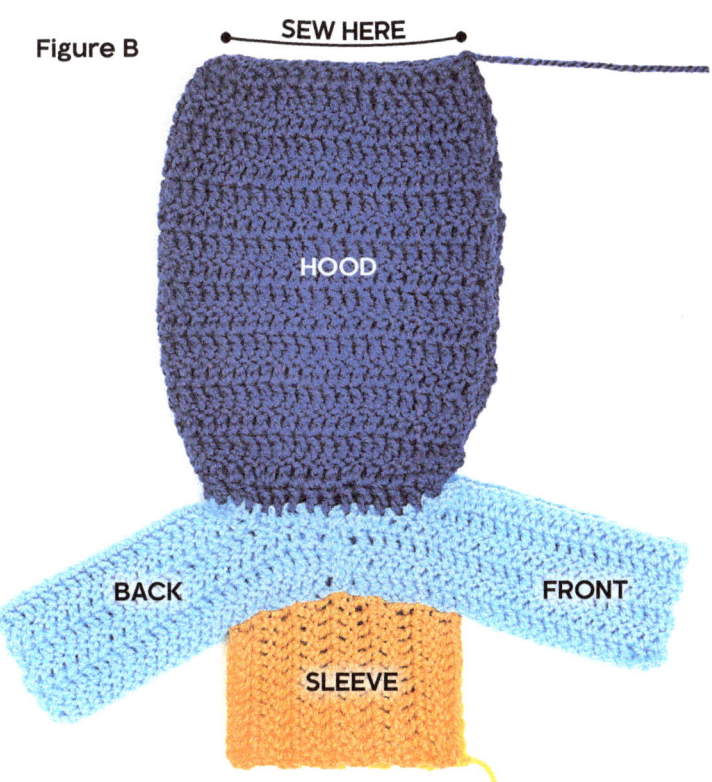

Sew fronts to back along underarms and sleeves. Turn cover-up right-side out.

Over-the-Rainbow Sundress

This pattern uses a combination of sc, hdc and dc, so be alert for stitch changes and color changes!

SUPPLIES

G6/4mm crochet hook

60 yds of DK, Light Worsted yarn in tangerine

Small amount of DK, Light Worsted yarn in purple, turquoise, green, yellow, orange & rose

Small hook and eye fastener

LIGHT 3

Note: A chain 1 at the beginning of a row is for turning your work and does not count as a stitch.

RAINBOW BODICE

With tangerine yarn, ch 2.

Row 1: 5 sc in 2nd ch from hook (5 sts).

Row 2: ch 1, turn, 2 sc in each st across; change to purple yarn in last st, cut off tangerine with 4-inch tail (10 sts).

Row 3: ch 1, turn, *sc in next st, 2 sc in next st* 5 times; change to turquoise yarn in last st, cut off purple with 4-inch tail (15 sts).

Row 4: ch 1, turn, **hdc** in each st across; change to green yarn in last st, cut off turquoise with 4-inch tail (15 sts).

Row 5: ch 1, turn, *sc in next st, 2 sc in next st* 3 times, sc in next 3 sts, *2 sc in next st, sc in next st* 3 times; change to yellow yarn in last st, cut off green with 4-inch tail (21 sts).

Row 6: ch 1, turn, **hdc** in each st across; change to orange yarn in last st, cut off yellow with 4-inch tail (21 sts).

Row 7: ch 1, turn, *sc in next 2 sts, 2 sc in next st* 3 times, sc in next 3 sts, *2 sc in next st, sc in next 2 sts* 3 times; change to rose yarn in last st, cut off orange with 4-inch tail (27 sts).

Row 8: ch 1, turn, **hdc** in each st across (27 sts).

Fasten off. Weave in ends.

SKIRT

Row 1: with tangerine yarn, ch 5, sc across straight side of bodice with 22 evenly-spaced sts, ch 5 (22 sts, 10 chs).

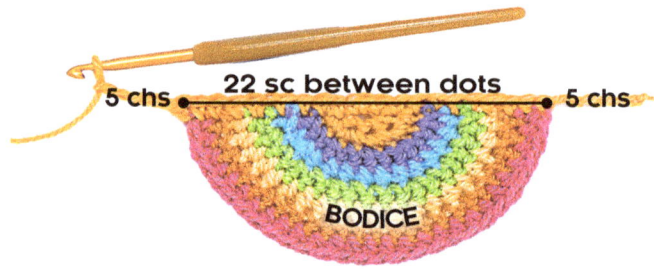

Row 2: ch 1, turn, dc in each st across (32 sts)

Row 3: ch 1, turn, 2 dc in each st across (64 sts).

Row 4: ch 1, turn, *dc in next st, 2 dc next st* across (96 sts).

Rows 5-7: ch 1, turn, dc in each st across; change to rose yarn in last st of Row 7.

Row 8: ch 1, turn, **hdc** in each st across.

FINISHING

Referring to Fig. A, bring dotted lines together and sew about half way up back edges of skirt. Sew hook and eye fastener at dots W and X.

For **neck ties**, using rose yarn, chain 2 strings making each 8 inches long. Sew ties to bodice at dots Y and Z.

Weave in ends. ♥

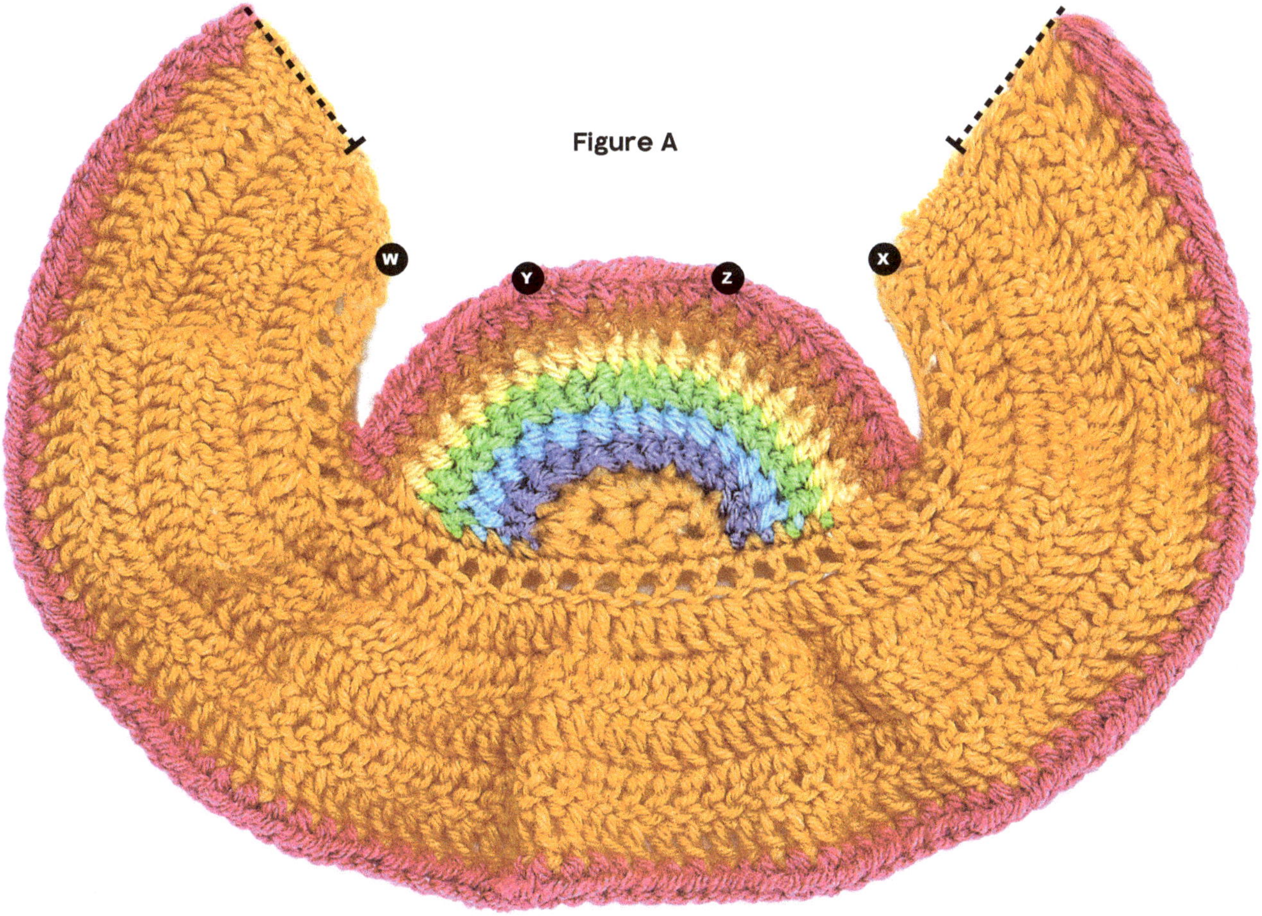

Figure A

DRESS BACK

BLUE VARIATION

Under-the-Sea Sundress

The dress is worked from the top down—starting with rows, then changing to rounds. Watch for the change to dc in Row 5. Final embellishments include appliques and beads. For a sweet, simple sundress, leave it unadorned.

SUPPLIES

LIGHT 3

G6/4mm and F5/3.75mm crochet hooks

Small amount of DK, Light Worsted yarn in lavender, pink & green

7 pearl beads, assorted sizes

1 black bead, 3mm

1 button, 1/2"

Sewing thread

Notes:
- A chain 1 at the beginning of a row is for turning your work and does not count as a stitch.
- When instructed to "crochet into the chain space" for Row 3, just insert your hook into the space underneath the chain to make your stitch. For a video demo, visit my Pinterest board of Amigurumi Tutorials (see page 93).

With lavender yarn and G6/4mm crochet hook, leaving a 12" starting tail, ch 33.

Row 1: sc in 2nd ch from hook and each remaining ch across (32 sts).

Row 2: ch 1, turn, sc in next 4 sts; for **armhole**, ch 6, skip next 8 sts; sc in next 8 sts; for **armhole**, ch 6, skip next 8 sts; sc in next 4 sts (16 sts, 12 chs).

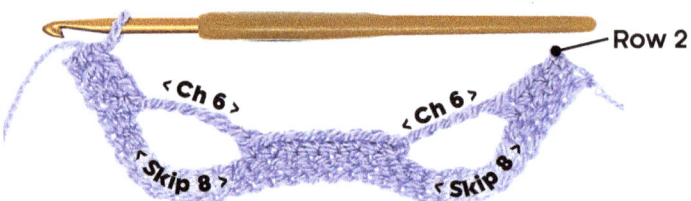

Row 3: ch 1, turn, sc in next 4 sts, 6 sc into chain space, sc in next 8 sts, 6 sc into chain space, sc in next 4 sts (28 sts).

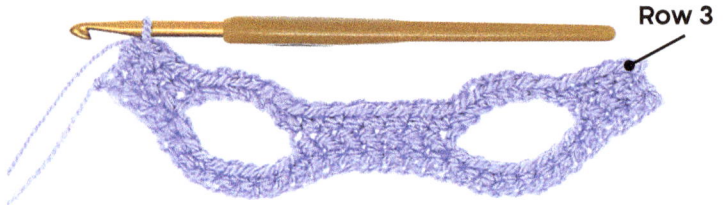

Row 4: ch 1, turn, sc in each st across (28 sts).

Row 5: ch 1, turn, *dc in next 6 sts, 2 dc in next st* 4 times, join with **sl st** in first st (32 sts).

Note: Now work in rnds. Place marker for beginning of rnd and move marker up as each rnd is completed.

Rnd 6: ch 1, starting in same st as where you made the **sl st**, *dc in next 7 sts, 2 dc in next st* 4 times, join with **sl st** in first st (36 sts).

Rnd 7: ch 1, starting in same st as where you made the **sl st**, *dc in next 8 sts, 2 dc in next st* 4 times, join with **sl st** in first st (40 sts).

Rnd 8: ch 1, starting in same st as where you made the **sl st**, *dc in next 9 sts, 2 dc in next st* 4 times, join with **sl st** in first st (44 sts).

Rnd 9: ch 1, starting in same st as where you made the **sl st**, *dc in next 10 sts, 2 dc in next st* 4 times, join with **sl st** in first st (48 sts).

Rnd 10: ch 1, starting in same st as where you made the **sl st**, *dc in next 11 sts, 2 dc in next st* 4 times, join with **sl st** in first st (52 sts).

Rnd 11: ch 1, starting in same st as where you made the **sl st**, *dc in next 12 sts, 2 dc in next st* 4 times, join with **sl st** in first st (56 sts).

Rnd 12: ch 1, starting in same st as where you made the **sl st**, *dc in next 13 sts, 2 dc in next st* 4 times, join with **sl st** in first st (60 sts).

Rnds 13-16: ch 1, starting in same st as where you made the **sl st**, *dc in each st around, join with **sl st** in first st.

Fasten off.

FISH APPLIQUE

The fish is worked around a foundation chain.

With F5/3.75mm crochet hook and pink yarn, ch 7.

Rnd 1: for **first side of fish**, sl st in 2nd ch from hook, hdc in next st, dc in next 2 sts, hdc in next st, sc in last st;

continue working forward around the chain,

for **second side of fish**, sc in next st, hdc in next st, dc in next 2 sts, hdc in next st, sl st in next st (12 sts).

Next a forked fin is worked in rows.

Row 2: for **first fork of fin**, ch 3, hdc in 2nd ch from hook, sc in next st, sl st in next st (3 sts).

Row 3: for **second fork of fin**, ch 3, hdc in 2nd ch from hook, sc in next st, sl st in next st (3 sts).

Fasten off. Thread ending tail into yarn needle and sew a stitch or two thru back of fish to close up the little hole where fin meets body. Weave in ends. Trim yarn tails. Pinch, push and pull fish into shape as needed.

SEAWEED

With F5/3.75mm crochet hook and green yarn, ch 18.

Row 1: for **first branch**, turn, sl st in 2nd ch from hook and in each remaining ch across (17 sts).

Row 2: for **second branch**, ch 12, turn, sl st in 2nd ch from hook and in each remaining ch across (11 sts).

Fasten off.

FINISHING

Glue fish to dress as pictured. Sew black bead in place for fish eye.

Position seaweed as pictured and pull yarn tails thru to inside of dress. Glue in place, pushing long branch into a wavy shape.

Sew pearl beads to dress as pictured.

For **button loop**, insert hook in 1st st of Row 1 and pull up a loop of yarn from starting tail, ch 5, sl st in next st. Fasten off. Sew button to corner opposite button loop.

Weave in ends. ♥

Striped Sundress

SUPPLIES

G6/4mm crochet hook

Small amount of DK, Light Worsted yarn in dark pink & light pink

2 buttons, 1/2"

Sewing thread

Notes:

- A chain 1 at the beginning of a row is for turning your work and does not count as a stitch.
- When instructed to "crochet into the chain space" for Row 50, just insert your hook into the space underneath the chain to make your stitch. For a video demo, visit my Pinterest board of Amigurumi Tutorials (see page 93).

SKIRT

With dark pink yarn, leaving a 12" starting tail, ch 22.

Row 1: ch 1, turn, sl st in next st, sc in next st, hdc in next 10 sts, dc in next 10 sts (22 sts).

Row 2: ch 1, turn, dc in next 10 sts, hdc in next 10 sts, sc in next st, sl st in next st; change to light pink yarn in last st (22 sts).

Row 3: ch 1, turn, sl st in next st, sc in next st, hdc in next 10 sts, dc in next 10 sts (22 sts).

Row 4: ch 1, turn, dc in next 10 sts, hdc in next 10 sts, sc in next st, sl st in next st; change to dark pink yarn in last st (22 sts).

Rows 5-44: repeat rows 1-4.

Fasten off **light pink** yarn.

You will have a total of 11 dark pink stripes and 11 light pink stripes.

YOKE

Place stitch markers to divide top edge of skirt into 4 equal sections (see dots in photo below). This will help you distribute your stitches evenly in Row 45.

Join **dark pink** yarn at RIGHT marker (pull up a loop).

Row 45: ch 1, make 8 sc between each pair of markers for a total of 32 sts across (32 sts).

Rows 46-48: ch 1, turn, sc in each st across.

Next, the armholes are made.

Row 49: ch 1, turn, sc in next 4 sts; for **armhole**, ch 3, skip next 7 sts; sc in next 10 sts; for **armhole**, ch 3, skip next 7 sts; sc in next 4 sts (18 sts, 6 chs).

See Fig. A.

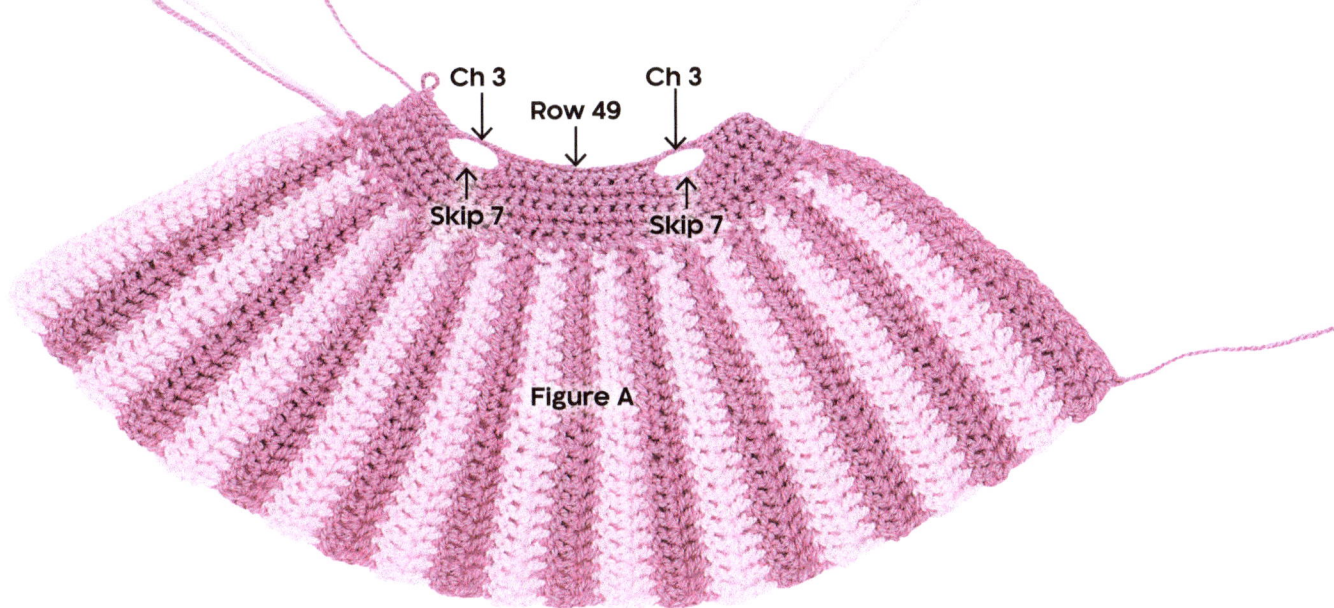

Figure A

Row 50: ch 1, turn, sc in next 4 sts, 5 sc into chain space, sc in next 10 sts, 5 sc into chain space, sc in next 4 sts (28 sts).

Row 51: for **1st button loop**, ch 4, do not turn, working along back edge of yoke, sc in each st until 1 st remains; for **2nd button loop**, ch 4, sc in last st of yoke. Fasten off.

For **button placket**, join with sc at lower edge of yoke on side opposite button loops.

Row 52: sc in each st across.

Row 53: ch 1, turn, sc in each sc across. Fasten off.

See Fig B.

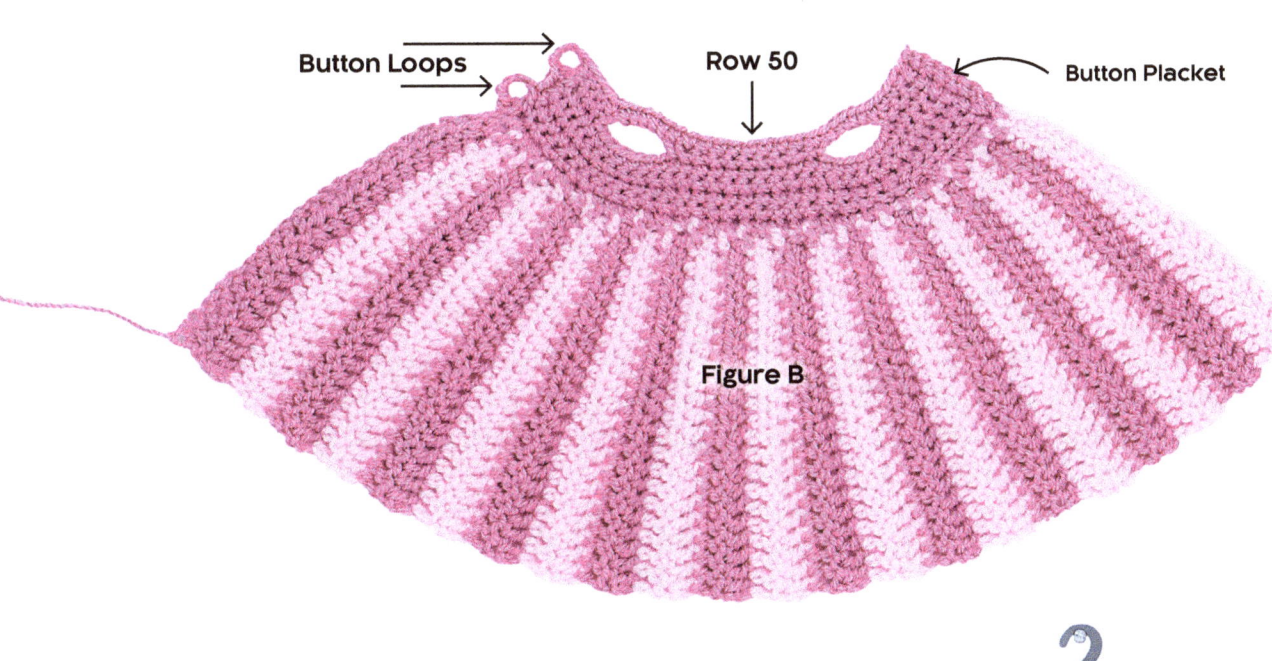

Figure B

FINISHING

Using long starting tail, sew skirt edges together for 3" up center back. Sew buttons to placket. Weave n ends. ♥

Starfish Sundress

Figure A

The Starfish Sundress is worked from the top down, starting with rows, then changing to rounds.

SUPPLIES

G6/4mm and E4/3.5mm crochet hooks

Small amount of DK, Light Worsted yarn in green & yellow

Button, 1/2"

Sewing thread

Note: A chain 1 at the beginning of a row is for turning your work and does not count as a stitch.

With G6/4mm crochet hook and yellow yarn, leaving a 12-inch starting tail, ch 25.

Row 1: sc in 2nd ch from hook and in each remaining ch across (24 sts).

Row 2: ch 1, turn, sc in next 4 sts; for **armhole**, ch 7, skip 3 sts; sc in next 10 sts; for **armhole**, ch 7, skip 3 sts; sc in next 4 sts (18 sts, 14 chs). See Fig. A.

Rows 3-9: ch 1, turn, sc in each st across; join end of Row 9 with **sl st** in first st, changing to green yarn in the sl st (32 sts).

Next work in joined rnds of **dc**. Place marker for beginning of rnd and move marker up as each rnd is completed.

Rnd 10: ch 1, starting in same st as where you made the **sl st**, 2 dc in each st around, join with **sl st** in first st (64 sts).

Rnd 11: ch 1, starting in same st as where you made the **sl st**, *dc in next st, 2 dc in next st* around, join with **sl st** in first st (96 sts).

Rnds 12-21: ch 1, starting in same st as where you made the **sl st**, dc in each st around, join with **sl st** in first st.

In the next rnd, the stitches are decreased to create a bubble skirt. Pull working yarn tight before each yarn over to gather the skipped stitch.

Rnd 22: ch 1 *skip 1 st, **sc** in next st* around (48 sts).

Rnd 23: sc in each st around.

Fasten off.

SMALL STARFISH APPLIQUE

With E4/3.5mm crochet hook and green yarn, ch 4 loosely, join with sl st in 1st st to make a **ring**. Note: Hold starting tail against ring and stitch over it when stitching into the ring.

Rnd 1: *ch 4, sl st in 2nd ch from hook, sl st in next ch, sl st into the **ring*** 5 times (5 arms).

Fasten off. Pull ring closed tight. Knot yarn tails together.

LARGE STARFISH APPLIQUE

With E4/3.5mm crochet hook and green yarn, ch 4 loosely, join with sl st in 1st st to make a **ring**. Note: Hold starting tail against ring and stitch over it when stitching into the ring.

Rnd 1: *ch 6, sl st in 2nd ch from hook, sl st in next ch, sc in next 2 chs, sl st into the **ring*** 5 times (5 arms).

Fasten off. Pull ring closed tight. Knot yarn tails together.

FINISHING

Sew or glue each starfish to dress as pictured.

For **button loop**, insert hook in 1st st of Row 1 and pull up a loop of yarn from starting tail, ch 5, sl st in next st. Fasten off. Sew button to corner opposite button loop.

Weave in ends. ♥

Basic Shirt

Make 2

FINISHING

Stack pieces and sew together across shoulders. Sew up sides leaving 1" open to make armholes. Weave in ends. ♥

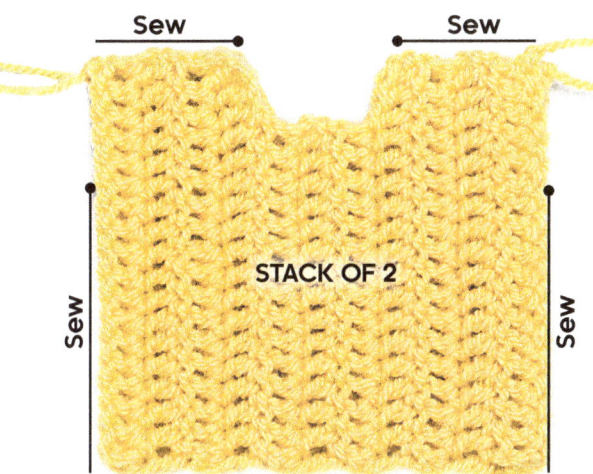

Sew   Sew
STACK OF 2
Sew   Sew

Two identical pieces are crocheted flat in rows and sewn together to make this easy shirt.

SUPPLIES

G6/4mm crochet hook

Small amount of DK, Light Worsted yarn

LIGHT 3

Note: A chain 1 at the beginning of a row is for turning your work and does not count as a stitch.

SHIRT (MAKE 2)

Ch 18.

Rows 1-4: ch 1, turn, dc in each st across (18 sts).

Rows 5-7: ch 1, turn, dc in next 15 sts (15 sts).

Row 8: ch 4, turn, dc in 2nd ch from hook and each remaining ch or st across (18 sts).

Rows 9-11: ch 1, turn, dc in each st across (18 sts).

Fasten off.

Crab Shirt

SUPPLIES

G6/4mm and F5/3.75mm crochet hooks

Small amount of DK, Light Worsted yarn in turquoise & red

2 black beads, 3mm

Sewing thread

Fabric glue (optional)

SHIRT

With G6/4mm crochet hook and turquoise yarn, follow instructions for Basic Shirt (see page 39).

CRAB APPLIQUE

With red yarn and F5/3.75mm crochet hook, make a magic ring, ch 1.

Rnd 1: 6 sc in ring, pull ring closed tight (6 sts).

Rnd 2: 2 sc in each st around. Place marker for beginning of rnd and move marker up as each rnd is completed (12 sts).

Rnd 3: *sc in next st, 2 sc in next st* 6 times (18 sts).

Rnd 4: *sc in next 2 sts, 2 sc in next st* 6 times (24 sts).

Next, the claws and legs will be created.

Rnd 5: for **1st claw**, ch 6, sl st in 2nd ch from hook, sl st in next 2 chs; **ch 3**, sl st in 2nd ch from hook, sl st in next ch; sl st in next 3 chs of main ch; sl st in next 2 sts of Rnd 4;

for **first 3 legs**, *ch 3, sl st in 2nd ch from hook, sl st in next ch, sl st in next 2 sts of Rnd 4* 3 times;

sl st in next 6 sts;

for **next 3 legs**, *ch 3, sl st in 2nd ch from hook, sl st in next ch, sl st in next 2 sts of Rnd 4* 3 times;

for **2nd claw**, ch 6, sl st in 2nd ch from hook, sl st in next 2 chs; **ch 3**, sl st in 2nd ch from hook, sl st in next ch; sl st in next 3 chs of main ch.

Sl st in next st. Fasten off. Weave in end.

FINISHING

Sew beads in place for eyes. Attach crab to shirt with sewing thread or glue. ♥

Sunshine Shirt

SUPPLIES

G6/4mm and F5/3.75mm crochet hooks

Small amount of DK, Light Worsted yarn in purple, yellow & orange

2 black beads, 3mm

Sewing thread

Fabric glue

Embroidery floss in black

Halter Top

SUPPLIES

G6/4mm crochet hook

Small amount of DK, Light Worsted yarn in turquoise, lavender, white, orange & rose

Notes:

• A chain 1 at the beginning of a row is for turning your work and does not count as a stitch.

• When instructed to crochet "in ch space", just insert your hook into the space underneath the chain. For a video demo, visit my Pinterest board of Amigurumi Tutorials (see page 93).

With turquoise yarn, ch 11.

Row 1: sc in 2nd ch from hook and in each remaining ch across; change to lavender yarn in last st (10 sts).

Row 2: ch 1, turn, sc in first 5 sts, ch 3, sc in last 5 sts (10 sts, 3 chs).

Row 3: ch 1, turn, sc in first 5 sts, (sc, ch 3, sc) in ch space, sc in last 5 sts; change to white yarn in last st (12 sts, 3 chs).

Row 4: ch 1, turn, sc in first 6 sts, (sc, ch 3, sc) in ch space, sc in last 6 sts (14 sts, 3 chs).

Row 5: ch 1, turn, sc in first 7 sts, (sc, ch 3, sc) in ch space, sc in last 7 sts; change to orange yarn in last st (16 sts, 3 chs).

Row 6: ch 1, turn, sc in first 8 sts, (sc, ch 3, sc) in ch space, sc in last 8 sts (18 sts, 3 chs).

Row 7: ch 1, turn, sc in first 9 sts, (sc, ch 3, sc) in ch space, sc in last 9 sts; change to rose yarn in last st (20 sts, 3 chs).

Row 8: ch 1, turn, sc in first 10 sts, (sc, ch 3, sc) in ch space, sc in last 10 sts (22 sts, 3 chs).

Row 9: ch 1, turn, sc in first 11 sts, (sc, ch 3, sc) in ch space, sc in last 11 sts; for **1st lower tie**, ch 50 (24 sts, 53 chs). Fasten off. Trim tail.

For **2nd lower tie**, join at other side of Row 9, ch 50. Fasten off. Trim tail.

Row 10: with turquoise yarn, for **1st upper tie**, ch 50; **sl st** into each st across neckline; for **2nd upper tie**, ch 50. Fasten off. Trim tails.

FINISHING

Weave in ends.

To make **fringe**, cut six 6-inch strands from each color. Alternating the colors, attach **2 strands** in every other stitch, plus the chain space, along Row 9. To attach fringe, put hook thru stitch, catch strands in the middle and pull part way thru stitch. Place tail ends over hook and pull them all the way thru loop on hook. Pull tails tight. Trim ends to 1 1/4". ♥

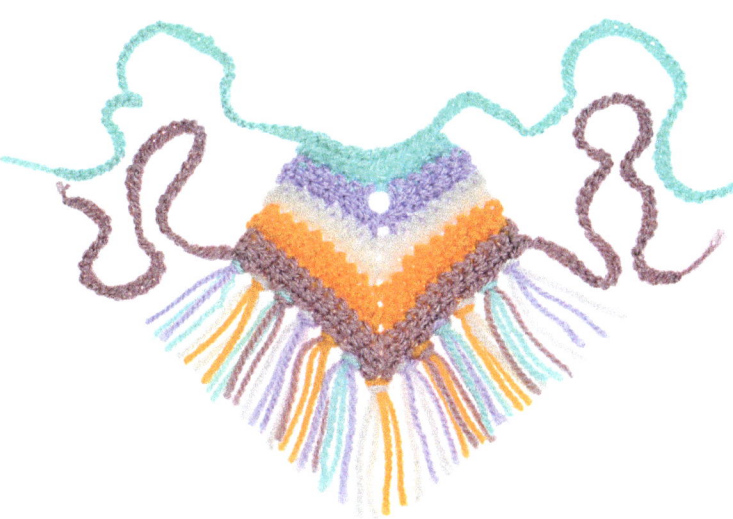

Polo Shirt

In this varitaion of the Basic Shirt, you will add stripes and a collar. Note that the stripe pattern on the back of the shirt is different than the front.

SUPPLIES

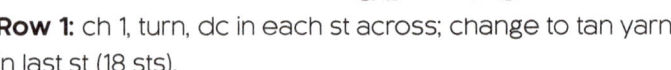

G6/4mm crochet hook

Small amount of DK, Light Worsted yarn in brown, tan, cream & blue

3 buttons, 1/4"

Sewing thread

Notes:

• A chain 1 at the beginning of a row is for turning your work and does not count as a stitch.

• After each color change, cut off old color leaving a 4" tail to be woven in later.

SHIRT FRONT

With tan yarn ch 18.

Rows 1-4: ch 1, turn, dc in each st across (18 sts).

Rows 5-6: ch 1, turn, dc in next 15 sts; change to cream yarn in last st of Row 6 (15 sts).

Row 7: ch 1, turn, dc in each st across (15 sts).

Row 8: ch 4, turn, dc in 2nd ch from hook and each remaining ch or st across; change to blue yarn in last st (18 sts).

Rows 9-10: ch 1, turn, dc in each st across; change to brown yarn in last st of Row 10 (18 sts).

Row 11: ch 1, turn, dc in each st across (18 sts).

Fasten off.

SHIRT BACK

With brown yarn ch 18.

Row 1: ch 1, turn, dc in each st across; change to tan yarn in last st (18 sts).

Rows 2-4: ch 1, turn, dc in each st across (18 sts).

Rows 5-7: ch 1, turn, dc in next 15 sts (15 sts).

Row 8: ch 4, turn, dc in 2nd ch from hook and each remaining ch or st across (18 sts).

Rows 9-11: ch 1, turn, dc in each st across (18 sts).

Fasten off.

Stack pieces so that brown edges meet and sew together across shoulders. For discreet sts across the striped shoulder, use invisible thread. Sew up sides leaving 1" open to make armholes.

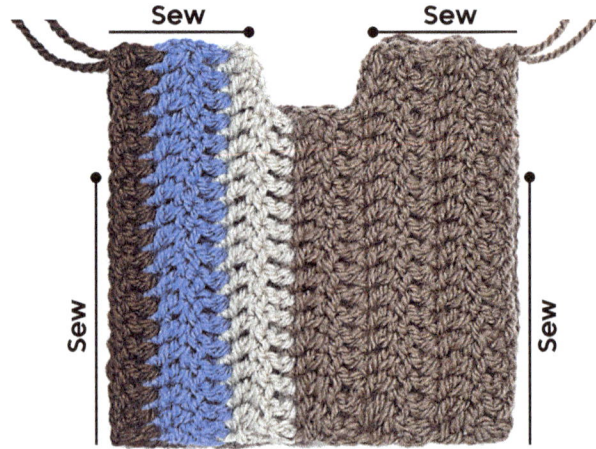

COLLAR

Join tan yarn with sc at center front of neckline.

Row 1: sc around neck edge to 1st st made.

Rows 2-4: ch 1, turn, sc in each st around. Fasten off.

FINISHING

Weave in ends. Sew buttons to center front as pictured. ♥

Button-Front Shirt

For this shirt, there will be a lot of ends to weave in — so turn on a good movie when it's time for finishing!

SUPPLIES

G6/4mm crochet hook

Small amount of DK, Light Worsted yarn in rust & gold

4 black buttons, 1/4"

Sewing thread

Notes:

• A chain 1 at the beginning of a row is for turning your work and does not count as a stitch.

• After each color change, cut off old color leaving a 4" tail to be woven in later.

SHIRT (MAKE 2)

With rust yarn, ch 18.

Row 1: ch 1, turn, dc in each st across; change to gold yarn in last st (18 sts).

Row 2: ch 1, turn, dc in each st across; change to rust yarn in last st (18 sts).

Row 3: ch 1, turn, dc in each st across; change to gold yarn in last st (18 sts).

Row 4: ch 1, turn, dc in each st across; change to rust yarn in last st (18 sts).

Row 5: ch 1, turn, dc in next 15 sts; change to gold yarn in last st (15 sts).

Row 6: ch 1, turn, dc in each st across; change to rust yarn in last st (15 sts).

Row 7: ch 1, turn, dc in each st across; change to gold yarn in last st (15 sts).

Row 8: ch 4, turn, dc in 2nd ch from hook and each remaining ch or st across; change to rust yarn in last st (18 sts).

Row 9: ch 1, turn, dc in each st across; change to gold yarn in last st (18 sts).

Row 10: ch 1, turn, dc in each st across; change to rust yarn in last st (18 sts).

Row 11: ch 1, turn, dc in each st across (18 sts).

Fasten off. Weave in ends.

Stack pieces with back sides facing and sew together across shoulders. For discreet sts across the striped shoulders, use invisible thread. Sew up sides leaving 1" open to make armholes.

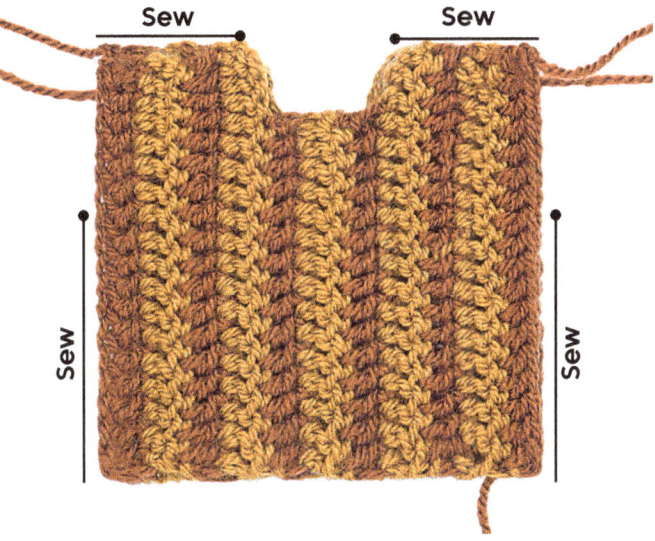

COLLAR

Join rust yarn with sc at center front of neckline.

Row 1: sc around neck edge to 1st st made.

Row 2: ch 1, turn, sc in each st around; change to gold yarn in last st.

Rows 3-4: ch 1, turn, sc in each st around. Fasten off.

FINISHING

Weave in ends. Sew buttons to center front as pictured. ♥

Shorts

Starting at the waist, this pattern is crocheted in joined rounds of hdc. Be sure to use stitch markers to keep track. I like to use bobby pins. These shorts are designed to fit snugly at the waist with no need for elastic. Choose between a short length for Summer and a longer version for Sunny.

SUPPLIES

G6/4mm crochet hook

Small amount of DK, Light Worsted yarn

Note: A chain 1 at the beginning of a round does not count as a stitch.

UPPER SHORTS

Ch 30, join with sl st in 1st ch to make a ring using care not to twist the chain.

Rnds 1-6: ch 1, hdc in each st around, sl st in 1st hdc to join the rnd. Place marker for beginning of rnd and move marker up as each rnd is completed (30 sts).

Crotch: ch 5, skip 14 sts, sl st in next st. This divides Rnd 6 for making pant legs. See Fig. A.

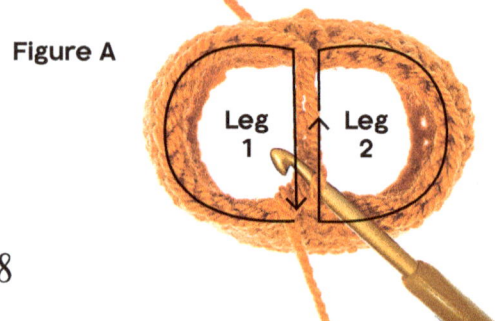

Figure A

LEG 1

Work as shown in Fig. A.

Rnds 7-10: ch 1, hdc in each st around, sl st in 1st hdc to join the rnd (20 sts).

Fasten off for Summer's shorts.

Rnds 11-12: ch 1, hdc in each st around, sl st in 1st hdc to join the rnd (20 sts).

Fasten off for Sunny's shorts.

LEG 2

Work as shown in Fig. A. Join with sl st at crotch.

Rnds 1-4: ch 1, hdc in each st around, sl st in 1st hdc to join the rnd (20 sts).

Fasten off for Summer's shorts.

Rnds 5-6: ch 1, hdc in each st around, sl st in 1st hdc to join the rnd (20 sts).

Fasten off for Sunny's shorts.

Weave in ends. ♥

Jeans Shorts

Make Shorts pattern with blue yarn. To finish, thread a blunt yarn needle with gold yarn. Sew around edges of legs and waist as pictured: Use a running stitch (see page 92) and push needle up and down thru holes between hdc stitches. Weave in ends. ♥

Jeans Skirt

The skirt is made from the top down. The pattern starts with rows to make a waistband with an opening at the back. The lower section is then made with joined rounds.

SUPPLIES

G6/4mm crochet hook

52 yds of DK, Light Worsted yarn in blue

Small amount of DK, Light Worsted yarn in gold

Button, 1/2"

Sewing thread

Note: A chain 1 at the beginning of a row or rnd does not count as a stitch.

SKIRT

Leaving a 12" starting tail, ch 30 with blue yarn.

Rows 1-4: ch 1, turn, hdc in each st across (30 sts).

Row 5: ch 1, turn, 2 dc in each st across; sl st to first st to join (60 sts).

Now work in joined rounds.

Rnds 6-11: ch 1, do not turn, dc in each st around; sl st to first st to join.

Fasten off.

FINISHING

For **button loop**, insert hook in 1st st of Row 1 and pull up a loop of yarn from starting tail, ch 3, sl st in next st. Fasten off.

For **decorative topstitching**, thread a blunt yarn needle with gold yarn. Sew thru starting chain, Rnd 1 and Rnd 11 as pictured: Use a running stitch (see page 92) and push needle up and down thru holes in stitches.

Sew **button** to corner opposite button loop.

Weave in ends. ♥

Shortalls

SUPPLIES

G6/4mm crochet hook

Small amount of DK, Light Worsted yarn in blue & white

2 buttons, 3/8"

Sewing thread

Note: A chain 1 at the beginning of a row is for turning your work and does not count as a stitch.

SHORTS

With blue yarn, ch 36, join with sl st to 1st ch to make a ring using care not to twist the chain.

Rnds 1-3: sc in each st around. Place marker for beginning of rnd and move marker up as each rnd is completed (36 sts).

Rnd 4: *sc in next 5 sts, 2 sc in next st* 6 times (42 sts).

Rnds 5-6: sc in each st around; change to white yarn in last st of Rnd 6.

Rnd 7: sc in each st around.

Rnd 8: *sc in next 6 sts, 2 sc in next st* 6 times; change to blue yarn in last st (48 sts).

Rnds 9-10: sc in each st around; change to white yarn in last st of Rnd 10.

Rnds 11-12: sc in each st around; change to blue yarn in last st of Rnd 12.

Rnds 13-14: sc in each st around; change to white yarn in last st of Rnd 14.

Rnds 15-16: sc in each st around; change to blue yarn in last st of Rnd 16.

Rnds 17-18: sc in each st around.

Crotch: ch 2, skip 23 sts, sc in next st. This divides Rnd 18 for making pant legs.

FIRST LEG

Rnd 19: sc in next 24 sts, sc in back loops of next 2 chs (26 sts).

Rnds 20-21: sc in each st around.

Sl st in next st. Fasten off.

SECOND LEG

Rnd 1: join with sc at remaining leg opening, sc in each st around. Place marker for beginning of rnd and move marker up as each rnd is completed (26 sts).

Rnds 2-3: sc in each st around.

Sl st in next st. Fasten off.

BIB

At upper edge of shorts, mark the 14 sts at center front for bib.

Row 1: join blue yarn with sc at right marker, sc in next 13 sts (14 sts).

Row 2: ch 1, turn, sc2tog, sc in next 10 sts, sc2tog (12 sts).

Row 3: ch 1, turn, sc2tog, sc in next 8 sts, sc2tog (10 sts).

Row 4: ch 1, turn, sc2tog, sc in next 6 sts, sc2tog (8 sts). Fasten off.

STRAPS (MAKE 2)

With blue yarn, ch 21; for **buttonhole**, skip first 4 chs from hook; sc in last 17 chs. Fasten off.

FINISHING

Sew buttons to corners of bib and attach straps with buttonholes. Sew back of straps to back of shortalls spaced 1 1/2" apart, crossing straps as shown in photo. Sew straps together at the X where they cross.

Weave in ends. ♥

Beach Pants

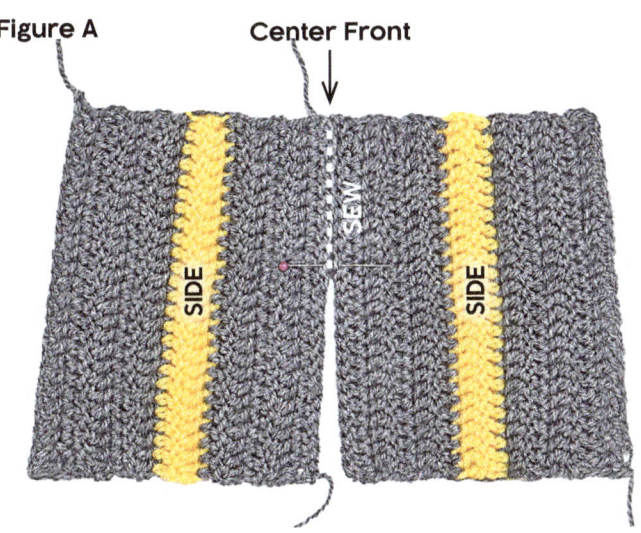
Figure A — Center Front — SEW — SIDE — SIDE

WAISTBAND

With G6/4mm crochet hook and gray yarn, join with sc at center back.

Rnds 1-2: sc in each st around.

Fasten off. Weave in ends.

FINISHING

Thread a yarn needle with elastic cord and weave thru back of stitches around waistband. Try pants on doll to

For a variation, omit the stripes to make solid-colored pants.

SUPPLIES

G6/4mm crochet hooks

Small amount of DK, Light Worsted yarn in gray & yellow

Stretch Magic clear elastic bead cord (.7mm)

Note: A chain 1 at the beginning of a row is for turning your work and does not count as a stitch.

SIDES (MAKE 2)

With gray yarn, ch 25 loosely.

Rows 1-5: ch 1, turn, dc in each st across; change to yellow yarn in last st of Row 5 (25 sts).

Rows 6-7: ch 1, turn, dc in each st across; change to gray yarn in last st of Row 7.

Rows 8-12: ch 1, turn, dc in each st across.

Fasten off.

Place pieces side-by-side (refer to Fig. A). For **center front** seam, sew top 10 sts together. Repeat for **center back** seam. To form **legs**, sew first and last rows together on each side.

51

Pajamas

Figure A

Fold work in half crosswise and sew up sides leaving 1" free at top to create armholes. See Fig. B.

Choose 2 colors of yarn for each set of pajamas. Use invisible sewing thread when you assemble the pieces to keep your stitches discreet. Elastic bead cord makes terrific waistband elastic.

SUPPLIES

G6/4mm crochet hook

Small amount of DK, Light Worsted yarn (2 colors per set)

Stretch Magic clear elastic bead cord (.7mm)

Invisible sewing thread

Note: A chain 1 at the beginning of a row is for turning your work and does not count as a stitch.

SHIRT SIDES (MAKE 2)

Make each panel a different color.

Ch 36.

Rows 1-5: ch 1, turn, dc in each st across (36 sts).

Row 6: ch 1, turn, **sc** in each st across. Fasten off.

Weave in ends.

Lay pieces side-by-side so rows of sc meet. Sew 12 of the sc stitches together at each end, leaving 12 sc stitches unsewn at the center to create neck opening. See Fig. A.

Figure B

SHORTS SIDES (MAKE 2)

Make each panel a different color.

Ch 13.

Rows 1-12: ch 1, turn, dc in each st across (13 sts).

Fasten off.

Place pieces side-by-side. For **center front** seam, sew top 10 sts together (see photo below). Repeat for **center back** seam. To form **legs**, sew first and last rows together on each side.

For **waistband**, join with sc at center back.

Rnds 13-14: sc in each st around. Fasten off.

Weave in ends.

Thread a yarn needle with elastic cord and weave thru back of stitches around **waistband**. Try shorts on doll to get the right tension and knot ends of elastic together.

Pajama Shorts are done. ♥

Row 9: ch 1, turn, sc2tog (1 st).

Row 10: ch 1, turn, 2 sc in next st (2 sts).

Row 11: ch 1, turn, 2 sc in next 2 sts (4 sts).

Row 12: ch 1, turn, 2 sc in next st, sc in next 2 sts, 2 sc in next st (6 sts).

Row 13: ch 1, turn, 2 sc in next st, sc in next 4 sts, 2 sc in next st (8 sts).

Row 14: ch 1, turn, 2 sc in next st, sc in next 6 sts, 2 sc in next st (10 sts).

Row 15: ch 1, turn, 2 sc in next st, sc in next 8 sts, 2 sc in next st (12 sts).

Rows 16-18: ch 1, turn, sc in each st across.

Do not fasten off.

Fold underwear in half crosswise (see Fig. A).

Figure A

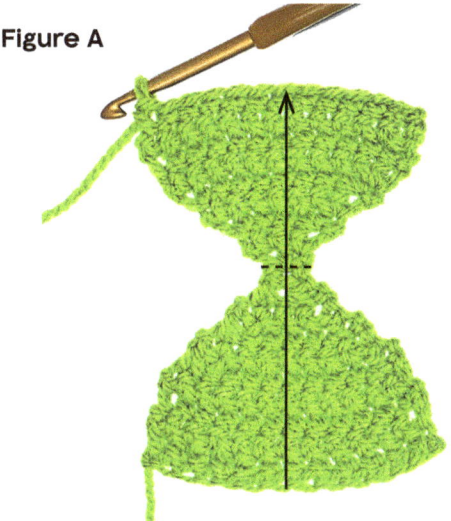

Underwear

SUPPLIES

G6/4mm crochet hook

Small amount of DK, Light Worsted yarn

Note: A chain 1 at the beginning of a row is for turning your work and does not count as a stitch.

Ch 13.

Row 1: sc in 2nd ch from hook and in each remaining ch across (12 sts).

Rows 2-3: ch 1, turn, sc in each st across.

Row 4: ch 1, turn, sc2tog, sc in next 8 sts, sc2tog (10 sts).

Row 5: ch 1, turn, sc2tog, sc in next 6 sts, sc2tog (8 sts).

Row 6: ch 1, turn, sc2tog, sc in next 4 sts, sc2tog (6 sts).

Row 7: ch 1, turn, sc2tog, sc in next 2 sts, sc2tog (4 sts).

Row 8: ch 1, turn, sc2tog twice (2 sts).

Rnds 19-20: sc in each st around (see Fig. B). This will connect front and back of underwear at waistline.

Figure B

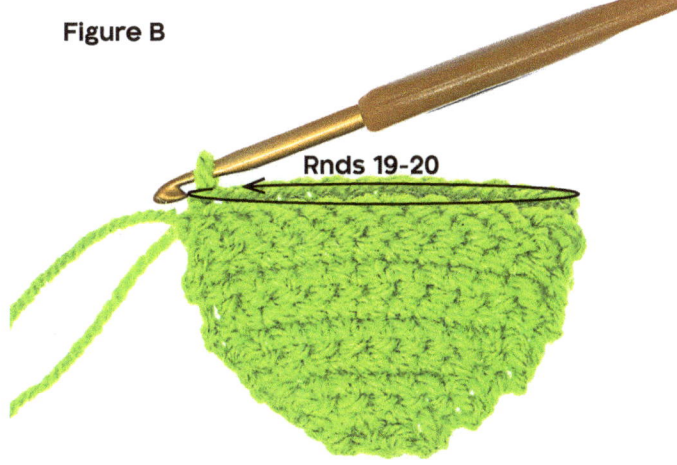

Sl st in next st. Fasten off.

Leg Trim: Work a round of sc around leg openings, joining the new yarn with sl st and ending with sl st.

Fasten off. Weave in ends. ♥

Cap

A button can be used to embellish the top of the cap as an alternative to the crocheted circle.

SUPPLIES

H8/5mm crochet hook

37 yds of Worsted weight yarn in blue

Small amount of Worsted weight yarn in rust

Fabric glue

MEDIUM 4

Note: A chain 1 at the beginning of a row is for turning your work and does not count as a stitch.

With blue yarn, make a magic ring, ch 1.

Rnd 1: 6 sc in ring, pull ring closed tight (6 sts).

Rnd 2: 2 sc in each st around. Place marker for beginning of rnd and move marker up as each rnd is completed (12 sts).

Rnd 3: *sc in next st, 2 sc in next st* 6 times (18 sts).

Rnd 4: *sc in next 2 sts, 2 sc in next st* 6 times (24 sts).

Rnd 5: *sc in next 3 sts, 2 sc in next st* 6 times (30 sts).

Rnd 6: *sc in next 4 sts, 2 sc in next st* 6 times (36 sts).

Rnd 7: *sc in next 5 sts, 2 sc in next st* 6 times (42 sts).

Rnd 8: *sc in next 6 sts, 2 sc in next st* 6 times (48 sts).

Rnds 9-14: sc in each st around.

Next, you will crochet in rows to make the **visor**.

Row 15: working in **front loops only**, sc2tog, *sc in next 2 sts, 2 sc in next st* 3 times, sc in next 2 sts, sc2tog (16 sts).

Row 16: ch 1, turn, resuming work in **both loops**, sc2tog, sc in next 12 sts, sc2tog (14 sts).

Row 17: ch 1, turn, sc2tog, sc in next 10 sts, sc2tog (12 sts).

Row 18: ch 1, turn, sc2tog, sc in next 8 sts, sc2tog (10 sts).

Fasten off.

For **edge trim**, join rust yarn at center back of cap.

Rnd 1: sc in each st around.

Rnd 2: **sl st** in each st around.

Fasten off. Weave in ends.

CIRCLE

With rust yarn, make a magic ring, ch 1.

Rnd 1: 6 sc in ring, pull ring closed tight (6 sts).

Fasten off. Sew ending tail down thru center "V" of next stitch to smooth the edge.

Position circle at top of cap. Pull yarn tails of circle to inside of cap and glue circle in place. Weave in ends. ♥

Sun Hat

The Sun Hat is worked from the top down in rounds. Worsted weight yarn gives it a sturdy structure.

SUPPLIES

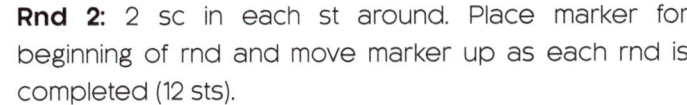

H8/5mm crochet hook

40 yds of Worsted weight yarn in light pink

Small amount of Worsted weight yarn in dark pink

With light pink yarn, make a magic ring, ch 1.

Rnd 1: 6 sc in ring, pull ring closed tight (6 sts).

Rnd 2: 2 sc in each st around. Place marker for beginning of rnd and move marker up as each rnd is completed (12 sts).

Rnd 3: *sc in next st, 2 sc in next st* 6 times (18 sts).

Rnd 4: *sc in next 2 sts, 2 sc in next st* 6 times (24 sts).

Rnd 5: *sc in next 3 sts, 2 sc in next st* 6 times (30 sts).

Rnd 6: *sc in next 4 sts, 2 sc in next st* 6 times (36 sts).

Rnd 7: *sc in next 5 sts, 2 sc in next st* 6 times (42 sts).

Rnd 8: *sc in next 6 sts, 2 sc in next st* 6 times (48 sts).

Rnds 9-10: sc in each st around; change to dark pink yarn in last st of Rnd 10.

Rnds 11-12: sc in each st around; change to light pink yarn in last st of Rnd 12.

Rnd 13: sc in each st around.

Next, the **brim** is made.

Rnd 14: working in **front loops only**, *sc in next 7 sts, 2 sc in next st* 6 times (54 sts).

Rnd 15: resuming work in **both loops**, *2 sc in next st, *sc in next 8 sts* 6 times (60 sts).

Rnd 16: *sc in next 9 sts, 2 sc in next st* 6 times; change to dark pink yarn in last st (66 sts).

Rnd 17: *2 sc in next st, sc in next 10 sts* 6 times (72 sts).

Rnd 18: sl st in each st around.

Fasten off. Weave in ends. ♥

Sandals

SUPPLIES

G6/4mm crochet hook

Small amount of DK Light Worsted yarn

Ch 15 loosely, join with sl st in 1st ch to make a ring using care not to twist the chain.

Rnds 1-2: sc in each st around (15 sts).

Now work in rows. A chain 1 at the beginning of a row is for turning your work and does not count as a stitch.

Row 3: sc in next 9 sts (9 sts).

Row 4: ch 1, turn, sc in next 9 sts (9 sts).

Row 5: ch 1, turn, sc2tog, sc in next 5 sts, sc2tog (7 sts).

Row 6: ch 1, turn, sc2tog, sc in next 3 sts, sc2tog (5 sts).

Now work in a round.

Rnd 7: ch 1, sc in each st around edge of sandal.

Sl st in next st. Fasten off. Weave in ends.

Make a second identical sandal. ♥

Beach Clogs

SUPPLIES

G6/4mm crochet hook

Small amount of DK Light Worsted yarn

Make a magic ring, ch 1.

Rnd 1: 5 sc in ring, pull ring closed tight (5 sts).

Rnd 2: 2 sc in each st around. Place marker for beginning of rnd and move marker up as each rnd is completed (10 sts).

Rnd 3: *sc in next st, 2 sc in next st* 5 times (15 sts).

Rnds 4-6: sc in each st around.

Now work in rows. A chain 1 at the beginning of a row is for turning your work and does not count as a stitch.

Row 7: sc in next 9 sts (9 sts).

Row 8: ch 1, turn, sc in next 9 sts (9 sts).

Row 9: ch 1, turn, sc2tog, sc in next 5 sts, sc2tog (7 sts).

Row 10: ch 1, turn, sc2tog, sc in next 3 sts, sc2tog (5 sts).

Now work in a round.

Rnd 11: ch 1, sc in each st around edge of clog.

Sl st in next st. Fasten off. Weave in ends.

Make a second identical clog. ♥

Sneakers

SUPPLIES

G6/4mm crochet hook

Small amount of DK, Light Worsted yarn in purple & white

With white yarn, make a magic ring, ch 1.

Rnd 1: 6 sc in ring, pull ring closed tight (6 sts).

Rnd 2: 2 sc in each st around. Place marker for beginning of rnd and move marker up as each rnd is completed (12 sts).

Rnd 3: *sc in next st, 2 sc in next st* 6 times (18 sts).

Rnd 4: *sc in next 2 sts, 2 sc in next st* 6 times (24 sts).

Rnd 5: sc in each st around; change to purple yarn in last st.

Rnd 6: *sc in next 2 sts, sc2tog* 6 times (18 sts).

Weave in loose tails now before shoe top gets too narrow.

Rnd 7: sc in next 6 sts, sc2tog 3 times, sc in next 6 sts (15 sts).

Rnd 8: sc in each st around.

Rnd 9: sl st in each st around. Fasten off. Weave in end.

Embroider laces as shown in photo.

Make a 2nd identical sneaker. ♥

Snug Boots

The boots have 2-layer soles. The bottom layer is worked separately in a lighter color and attached with slip stitch.

SUPPLIES

G6/4mm crochet hook

Small amount of DK Light Worsted yarn in gold and tan

Small amount of Bulky boucle yarn in cream

With gold yarn, ch 6. Next crochet around the chain.

Rnd 1: for **1st sole**, starting in 2nd ch from hook, sc in next 4 chs, 3 sc in next ch, sc in next 3 chs, 2 sc in last ch. Place marker for beginning of rnd and move marker up as each rnd is completed (12 sts).

Rnd 2: 2 sc in next st, sc in next 3 sts, 2 sc in next 3 sts, sc in next 3 sts, 2 sc in next 2 sts (18 sts).

Rnd 3: 2 sc in next st, sc in next 4 sts, 2 sc in next st, *sc in next st, 2 sc in next st* twice, sc in next 4 sts, *2 sc in next st, sc in next st* twice (24 sts).

Rnd 4: working in **back loops only**, sc in each st around.

Rnds 5-7: resuming work in **both loops**, sc in each st around.

Rnd 8: sc in next 8 sts, sc2tog 4 times, sc in next 8 sts (20 sts).

Rnd 9: sc in next 8 sts, sc2tog twice, sc in next 8 sts (18 sts).

Rnds 10-14: sc in each st around; change to cream yarn in last st of Rnd 14.

Rnd 15: working in **back loops only**, sc in each st around.

Fasten off. Weave in ends.

For **2nd sole**, use tan yarn and repeat **Rnds 1-3**. Do not fasten off. Place wrong side against bottom of boot with sts aligned. **Sl st** soles together working thru both loops of 2nd sole and unworked front loops of 1st sole. Fasten off. Weave in ends.

Make a second identical boot. ♥

57

Beach Play Mat

The Beach Play Mat is an easy-level pattern created with a combination of single crochet (sand) and a wavy stitch pattern of double crochet (ocean). A narrow wavy section of sea foam is created with white yarn.

If you have never crocheted a wave-type project, watching a video for an overview of the technique is helpful. There are many demos on YouTube. Just search YouTube for 'wave stitch crochet', 'ripple stitch crochet' or 'chevron stitch crochet' and choose a video featuring wide and gentle waves that look similar to this playmat.

If you are a beginner at the wave or ripple stitch, I also recommend starting with a small sample to get familiar with the technique. A chain of 36 + 2 for the turning chain (total 38), is a good size for a test swatch.

Notes:

• The **crest** is the highest part of a wave and the **trough** is the lowest part.

• Always mark the ch-2 that counts as 1st dc on Rows 2-46. You will need to work into this chain later and it can be tricky to locate. I like to mark it with a bobby pin.

• To **DC2TOG:** *Yarn over, insert hook in next st and pull up a loop, yarn over and pull thru 2 loops* _twice_, yarn over and pull thru all 3 loops on hook.

• The wave pattern is created by alternating crests of **2 dc in the same st** _twice_ and troughs of **dc2tog** _twice_. The crests and troughs are separated by 3 dc. The end of each row has a half-crest of 2 dc in the same st.

To help you check your work, the photo below shows how the stitches of the wave pattern look:

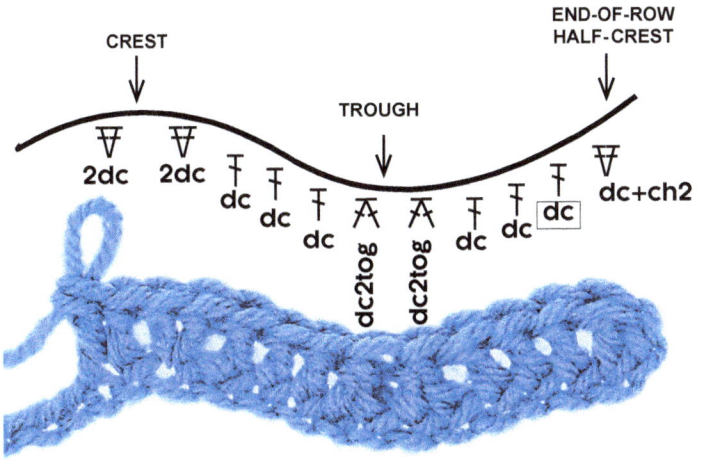

SUPPLIES

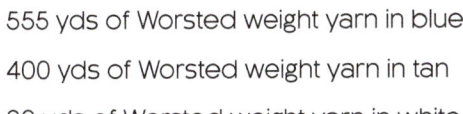

H8/5mm crochet hook

555 yds of Worsted weight yarn in blue

400 yds of Worsted weight yarn in tan

30 yds of Worsted weight yarn in white

SIZE ~ 24" x 40"

With blue yarn, ch 110.

Row 1: dc in 3rd ch from hook (2 skipped chs count as 1st dc), dc in next 3 chs, dc2tog _twice_, *dc in next 3 chs, 2 dc in next 2 chs, dc in next 3 chs, dc2tog _twice_* 8 times until 4 chs remain; dc in next 3 chs, 2 dc in last ch (108 sts).

Rows 2-46: ch **2** loosely (counts as 1st dc), turn, place stitch marker in the ch-2, working in **back loops only**, dc in SAME st as where your ch started, dc in next 3 sts, dc2tog _twice_, *dc in next 3 sts, 2 dc in next 2 sts, dc in next 3 sts, dc2tog _twice_* 8 times until 4 sts remain; dc in next 3 sts, 2 dc in last st; change to white yarn in last st of Row 46 (108 sts).

Rows 47-48: work the same as Row 2; change to tan yarn in last st of Row 48 (108 sts).

Row 49: ch **1** (counts as sl st), turn, working in **back loops only**, sc in NEXT st from where your ch started, hdc in next 3 sts, dc2tog, *hdc in next 3 sts, sc in next st, sl st loosely in next 2 sts, sc in next st, hdc in next 3 sts, dc2tog* 8 times until 5 sts remain; hdc in next 3 sts, sc in next st, sl st in last st (99 sts).

Rows 50-119: ch **1** (does not count as st), turn, working in **both loops**, sc in each st across (99 sts). Fasten off.

For your final row, the ocean end of the mat is straightened to fill in the troughs. With front of mat facing you, join blue yarn at right corner.

Row 120: ch **2** (counts as dc), hdc in next 3 sts, sc in next st, sl st in next 2 sts, *sc in next st, hdc in next 3 sts, dc in next 2 sts, hdc in next 3 sts, sc in next st, sl st in next 2 sts* 8 times until 5 sts remain; sc in next st, hdc in next 3 sts, dc in last st (108 sts).

Fasten off. Weave in ends. ♥

Tip: To make a bigger Beach Play Mat, make a longer starting chain. The wave pattern is worked in multiples of 12 (+ 2 for the turning chain).

Swim Ring

The swim ring is worked in rows, then sewn into a donut shape. Instructions are provided for a peach and red ring — but you can have fun playing with different color combinations.

Even the animals — Sandy, Seabert, Starla, Clawde and Ray — enjoy floating on the swim ring!

SUPPLIES

G6/4mm crochet hook

Small amount of Worsted weight yarn in peach & red

Polyester fiberfill stuffing

Notes:
- A chain 1 at the beginning of a row is for turning your work and does not count as a stitch.
- For color changes, carry unused color across ends of rows.

With peach yarn, ch 42.

Row 1: ch 1, turn, sc in each st across; change to red yarn in last st (42 sts).

Row 2: ch 1, turn, *sc in next 6 sts, 2 sc in next st* 6 times (48 sts).

Row 3: ch 1, turn, *sc in next 7 sts, 2 sc in next st* 6 times; change to peach yarn in last st (54 sts).

Rows 4-5: ch 1, turn, sc in each st across; change to red yarn in last st of Row 5 (54 sts).

Rows 6-7: ch 1, turn, sc in each st across; change to peach yarn in last st of Row 7 (54 sts).

Rows 8-9: ch 1, turn, sc in each st across; change to red yarn in last st of Row 9 (54 sts).

Row 10: ch 1, turn, sc in each st across.

Row 11: ch 1, turn, *sc in next 7 sts, sc2tog* 6 times; change to peach yarn in last st (48 sts).

Row 12: ch 1, turn, *sc in next 6 sts, sc2tog* 6 times (42 sts). Fasten off with extra long tail.

FINISHING

The piece will look like a letter C. Sew Rows 1 and 12 together with peach yarn tail to make a tube. Stuff the tube as you sew.

Bend the C into an O. Sew ends together using a peach yarn tail to connect the peach stripes and a red yarn tail to connect the red stripes.

Hide yarn tails inside. ♥

Beach Towel

The directions below are for a purple towel. Sunny's towel in shades of green is shown for inspiration.

SUPPLIES

MEDIUM 4

H8/5mm crochet hook
60 yds of Worsted weight yarn in purple
45 yds of Worsted weight yarn in lavender

Notes:
- A chain 1 at the beginning of a row is for turning your work and does not count as a stitch.
- For color changes, carry unused color along the edge.

With purple yarn, ch 42.

Rows 1-2: ch 1, turn, dc in each st across; change to lavender yarn in last st of Row 2 (42 sts).

Rows 3-4: ch 1, turn, dc in each st across; change to purple yarn in last st of Row 4.

Rows 5-6: ch 1, turn, dc in each st across; change to lavender yarn in last st of Row 6.

Rows 7-8 ch 1, turn, dc in each st across; change to purple yarn in last st of Row 8.

Rows 9-10: ch 1, turn, dc in each st across; change to lavender yarn in last st of Row 10.

Rows 11-12 ch 1, turn, dc in each st across; change to purple yarn in last st of Row 12.

Rows 13-14: ch 1, turn, dc in each st across.

Row 15: for **end trim**, ch 1, do not turn, **sc** across ends of rows making 4 sts across each stripe (28 sts).

Row 16: ch 1, turn, **sc** in each st across. Fasten off.

Rows 17-18: join purple yarn at other end of towel and work 2 rows of sc in same manner as Rows 15-16.

Fasten off. Weave in ends. ♥

Raft

The raft is made in 1 piece. The top is striped and the bottom is solid purple. You will need to change colors on the starting chain. To do this, simply release the working yarn of the current color, yarn over with the new color and pull the new color thru the loop on your hook. The use of invisible thread for finishing keeps the stitches hidden where different colors meet.

SUPPLIES

H8/5mm crochet hook

120 yds of Worsted weight yarn in purple

25 yds of Worsted weight yarn in green, orange & turquoise

Polyester fiberfill stuffing

Invisible sewing thread

Note: A chain 1 at the beginning of a row is for turning your work and does not count as a stitch.

With green yarn, ch 40; change to purple yarn, ch 60 (100 chs).

Row 1: ch 1, turn, sc in next 60 sts; change to green yarn, sc in next 40 sts (100 sts).

Row 2: ch 1, turn, sc in next 40 sts; change to purple yarn, sc in next 60 sts (100 sts).

Rows 3-8: repeat Rows 1-2. Cut off green yarn after Row 8.

Row 9: ch 1, turn, sc in next 60 sts; change to orange yarn, sc in next 40 sts (100 sts).

Row 10: ch 1, turn, sc in next 40 sts; change to purple yarn, sc in next 60 sts (100 sts).

Rows 11-16: repeat Rows 9-10. Cut off orange yarn after Row 16.

Row 17: ch 1, turn, sc in next 60 sts; change to turquoise yarn, sc in next 40 sts (100 sts).

Row 18: ch 1, turn, sc in next 40 sts; change to purple yarn, sc in next 60 sts (100 sts).

Rows 19-24: repeat Rows 17-18. Fasten off.

Weave in ends.

Refer to Fig. A for shape of work after Row 24.

Figure A

Figure B

FINISHING

Fold piece in half widthwise to look like Fig. B.

With invisible thread, sew left edges together with whip stitch (see black dotted line in Fig. B).

Sew thru both layers along white dotted line in Fig. B to create pillow. Stuff pillow.

Sew right edges together with whip stitch (see red dotted line in Fig. B).

Sew between stripes thru both layers to create tubes. Stuff tubes.

Sew layers of bottom edge together with whip stitch. ♥

Bottom of Raft

Bodyboard

SUPPLIES

H8/5mm crochet hook

60 yds of Worsted weight yarn in yellow

Small amount of Worsted weight yarn in black

Small piece of corrugated cardboard

2-hole black button, 1" diameter

BODYBOARD

With yellow yarn, make a magic ring, ch 1.

Rnd 1: 6 sc in ring, pull ring closed tight (6 sts).

Rnd 2: 2 sc in each st around. Place marker for beginning of rnd and move marker up as each rnd is completed (12 sts).

Rnd 3: *sc in next st, 2 sc in next st* 6 times (18 sts).

Rnd 4: *sc in next 2 sts, 2 sc in next st* 6 times (24 sts).

Rnd 5: *sc in next 3 sts, 2 sc in next st* 6 times (30 sts).

Rnds 6-29: sc in each st around.

Flatten piece with working yarn at right side. Cut a piece of cardboard using the template for a pattern. Insert cardboard in bodyboard.

Next, you will work a row to connect the bottom edges.

Row 30: ch 1, working thru both layers, sc in each st across (15 sts).

Row 31: ch 1, turn, dc in next st, hdc in next st, sc in next st, sl st in next 9 sts, sc in next st, hdc in next st, dc in last st (15 sts).

Fasten off. Weave in end.

LEASH

With black yarn, ch 30, skip first 10 chs from hook, **sl st** in last 20 chs. Fasten off.

Thread each yarn tail of leash thru a hole of your button. If the holes in your button are small, use this method to easily insert yarn thru a buttonhole: Cut a length of sewing thread about 12" long. Insert one end thru hole in button. Insert other end of sewing thread back thru same hole in button so that it forms a loop on one side and both ends are sticking out the other side. Insert yarn thru loop, then pull on ends of thread.

To attach button/leash assembly to bodyboard, use 1 yarn tail to sew a stitch thru top layer of fabric under Rnd 8. (Do not sew thru cardboard.) Knot both yarn tails together under button. To hide tails, sew them between layers of fabric and cardboard. ♥

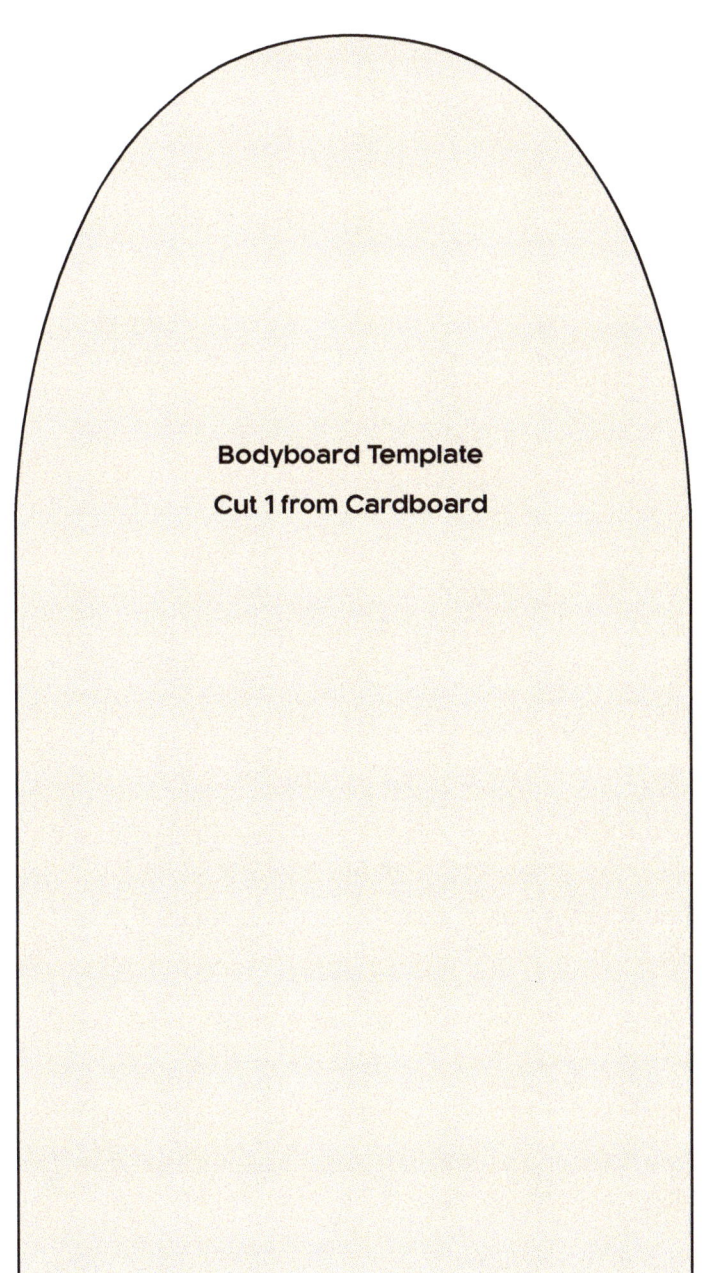

Bodyboard Template
Cut 1 from Cardboard

Beach Bucket

The bucket is especially fun for collecting clams and sand dollars. The movable handle has a buttonhole at each end for attaching it to the bucket.

SUPPLIES

G6/4mm crochet hook

Small amount of Worsted weight yarn in red & green

2 yellow buttons, 5/8" diameter

Sewing thread

Small piece of thin rigid plastic (milk jug or food packaging)

BUCKET

With red yarn, make a magic ring, ch 1.

Rnd 1: 6 sc in ring, pull ring closed tight (6 sts).

Rnd 2: 2 sc in each st around. Place marker for beginning of rnd and move marker up as each rnd is completed (12 sts).

Rnd 3: *sc in next st, 2 sc in next st* 6 times (18 sts).

Rnd 4: *sc in next 2 sts, 2 sc in next st* 6 times (24 sts).

Rnd 5: *sc in next 3 sts, 2 sc in next st* 6 times (30 sts).

Rnd 6: working in **back loops only**, sc in each st around.

Rnd 7: resuming work in **both loops**, sc in each st around.

Rnd 8: *sc in next 14 sts, 2 sc in next st* twice (32 sts).

Rnd 9: sc in each st around.

Rnd 10: *sc in next 15 sts, 2 sc in next st* twice (34 sts).

Rnd 11: sc in each st around.

Rnd 12: *sc in next 16 sts, 2 sc in next st* twice (36 sts).

Rnd 13: sc in each st around.

Rnd 14: *sc in next 17 sts, 2 sc in next st* twice (38 sts).

Rnd 15: sc in each st around.

Rnd 16: *sc in next 18 sts, 2 sc in next st* twice (40 sts).

Rnd 17: sc in each st around.

Rnd 18: sl st in each st around.

Fasten off. Weave in ends.

HANDLE

With green yarn, ch 30. For **buttonhole**, skip first 5 chs from hook, sc in last 25 chs; for second **buttonhole**, ch 4, fasten off and tie tails together. Weave in ends.

FINISHING

Sew a button to each side of bucket at rim. Use buttonholes to attach handle to bucket.

Cut a 2-inch diameter circle of thin plastic (see Bucket Base Template below). Insert in bottom of bucket. ♥

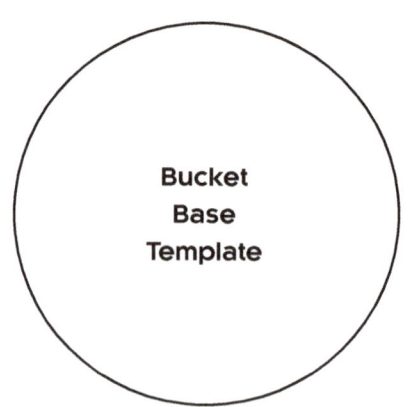

Sand Shovel

A dab of glue keeps a wooden skewer inside the handle from poking thru the crochet during play.

SUPPLIES

G6/4mm crochet hook

Small amount of Worsted weight yarn

Bamboo skewer

White glue

BLADE

Leaving a 12-inch starting tail, ch 16; join with sl st to first ch to make a ring using care not to twist the chain.

Rnd 1: sc in each ch around. Place marker for beginning of rnd and move marker up as each rnd is completed (16 sts).

Rnds 2-7: ch 1, turn, sc in each st around.

Flatten blade with working yarn at right side. Next you will close up the end.

Row 8: ch 1, working thru both layers, sc in each st across (8 sts).

Fasten off.

HANDLE

Make a magic ring, ch 1.

Rnd 1: 6 sc in ring, pull ring closed tight (6 sts).

Rnds 2-15: sc in each st around. Place marker for beginning of rnd and move marker up as each rnd is completed.

Fasten off.

FINISHING

Dip blunt end of skewer in white glue and scrape off the excess. Insert blunt end in handle and cut skewer to fit length of handle. Sew open end of handle shut. Slide handle all the way into blade until it touches end of blade.

Using starting tail, sew upper edge of blade closed, sewing handle to blade as you work.

Weave in ends. ♥

Beach Ball

SUPPLIES

G6/4mm crochet hook

Small amount of Worsted weight yarn in pink, turquoise, yellow, green, orange and purple

Invisible sewing thread

Polyester fiberfill stuffing

Note: A chain 1 at the beginning of a row is for turning your work and does not count as a stitch.

PANELS (MAKE 6)

Make 1 panel in each color.

Row 1: ch 2, sc in 2nd ch from hook (1 st).

Row 2: ch 1, turn, 2 sc in next st (2 sts).

Row 3: ch 1, turn, sc in next st, 2 sc in next st (3 sts).

Row 4: ch 1, turn, sc in next st, 2 sc in next st, sc in next st (4 sts).

Row 5: ch 1, turn, sc in next 2 sts, 2 sc in next st, sc in next st (5 sts).

Row 6: ch 1, turn, sc in next 2 sts, 2 sc in next st, sc in next 2 sts (6 sts).

Row 7: ch 1, turn, sc in next 3 sts, 2 sc in next st, sc in next 2 sts (7 sts).

Rows 8-13: ch 1, turn, sc in each st across.

Row 14: ch 1, turn, sc in next 3 sts, sc2tog, sc in next 2 sts (6 sts).

Row 15: ch 1, turn, sc in next 2 sts, sc2tog, sc in next 2 sts (5 sts).

Row 16: ch 1, turn, sc in next 2 sts, sc2tog, sc in next st (4 sts).

Row 17: ch 1, turn, sc in next st, sc2tog, sc in next st (3 sts).

Row 18: ch 1, turn, sc in next st, sc2tog (2 sts).

Row 19: ch 1, turn, sc2tog (1 st).

Fasten off. Weave in ends.

FINISHING

Holding 2 panels with right sides facing, sew the edges together using invisible sewing thread. Continue sewing panels together until you get to the final seam. Pause when half-way across to turn ball right-side out and stuff it firmly. Finishing sewing ball closed. Be sure to sew across top and bottom of ball securely where all 6 panels meet.

Squeeze ball into shape. ♥

Mini FrizzBee

A beach party isn't complete without a frizzbee! This doll-size disc (3" dia) soars just like a full-size one. It's safe for indoors and your pets will love it, too. In this pattern, you will be working with 2 strands of yarn held together. If you've never crocheted with multiple strands, just pretend you are working with a single strand and make each stitch as if you were holding 1 strand of yarn.

SUPPLIES

H8/5mm crochet hook

Small amount of Worsted weight yarn

Note: Hold 2 strands of yarn together for the entire pattern.

Ch 10, join with sl st to first ch to make a **ring** using care not to twist the chain.

Rnd 1: 18 sc in **ring** (18 sts).

Rnd 2: *sc in next 2 sts, 2 sc in next st* 6 times. Place marker for beginning of rnd and move marker up as each rnd is completed (24 sts).

Rnd 3: *sc in next st, 2 sc in next st, sc in next 2 sts* 6 times (30 sts).

Rnd 4: *sc in next 3 sts, 2 sc in next st, sc in next st* 6 times (36 sts).

Rnd 5: sc in each st around.

Rnd 6: sl st in each st around.

Fasten off. Weave in ends. ♥

Sunscreen Lotion

SUPPLIES

F5/3.75mm crochet hook

Small amount of DK, Light Worsted yarn in blue, orange & turquoise

Small piece of thin cardboard (cereal box weight)

Polyester fiberfill stuffing

With blue yarn, make a magic ring, ch 1.

Rnd 1: 4 sc in ring, pull ring closed tight (4 sts).

Rnd 2: 2 sc in each st around. Place marker for beginning of rnd and move marker up as each rnd is completed (8 sts).

Rnd 3: 2 sc in each st around (16 sts).

Rnd 4: working in **back loops only**, sc in each st around.

Rnds 5-7: resuming work in **both loops**, sc in each st around; change to orange yarn in last st of Rnd 7.

For **lid liner**, cut a 1" circle of thin cardboard by tracing a U.S. quarter or using the template below. Insert inside lid to keep top flat.

Rnds 8-12: sc in each st around; change to turquoise yarn in last st of Rnd 12.

Rnds 13-15: sc in each st around; change to orange yarn in last st of Rnd 15.

Rnds 16-20: sc in each st around.

Stuff tube. Flatten with working yarn at right corner. Next, you will close up the end.

Row 21: ch 1, working thru both layers, sc in each st across (8 sts).

Fasten off. Hide tail inside. ♥

67

Clams

The little clams feature a pearl inside for a fun surprise.

SUPPLIES

F5/3.75mm crochet hook

Small amount of DK, Light Worsted yarn in gray & peach

Pearl bead, 8mm

Sewing thread

White glue

OUTER SHELLS (MAKE 2)

With gray yarn, make a magic ring, ch 1.

Rnd 1: 6 sc in ring, pull ring closed tight (6 sts).

Rnd 2: 2 sc in each st around. Place marker for beginning of rnd and move marker up as each rnd is completed (12 sts).

Rnd 3: *sc in next st, 2 sc in next st* 6 times (18 sts).

Rnd 4: *sc in next 2 sts, 2 sc in next st* 6 times (24 sts).

Rnd 5: *sc in next 11 sts, 2 sc in next st* twice (26 sts).

Rnd 6: sl st in each st around.

Fasten off.

INNER SHELLS (MAKE 2)

With peach yarn, make a magic ring, ch 1.

Rnd 1: 6 sc in ring, pull ring closed tight (6 sts).

Rnd 2: 2 sc in each st around. Place marker for beginning of rnd and move marker up as each rnd is completed (12 sts).

Rnd 3: *sc in next st, 2 sc in next st* 6 times (18 sts).

Sl st in next st. Fasten off.

FINISHING

Sew pearl bead to center of one inner shell.

Nest inner shells inside outer shells with wrong sides facing and glue in place.

Place shells together with peach sides facing. Sew rims of outer shells together with 5 whip stitches to make a hinge. Secure with a knot.

Weave in ends. ♥

Sand Dollars

The sand dollars are fun to collect in the beach bucket. Patterns are provided for 2 sizes.

SUPPLIES

G6/4mm crochet hook

Small amount of Worsted weight yarn in off-white

SMALL SAND DOLLAR

Make a magic ring, ch 1.

Rnd 1: 6 sc in ring, pull ring closed tight (6 sts).

Rnd 2: 2 sc in each st around. Place marker for beginning of rnd and move marker up as each rnd is completed (12 sts).

Rnd 3: *sc in next st, 2 sc in next st* 6 times (18 sts).

Rnd 4: sc in each st around.

Rnd 5: *sc in next st, sc2tog* 6 times (12 sts).

Rnd 6: sc2tog 6 times (6 sts).

Fasten off with extra long tail. To close hole, thread tail in yarn needle, insert needle thru front loop of each st around opening & pull tight. Sew tail up thru center of Rnd 6 and out at center of Rnd 1. Embroider surface of sand dollar with 5 Lazy Daisy stitches as pictured. Be sure to keep back side of embroidery sts hidden between layers of sand dollar. Hide remaining tail inside.

Tip: Mark location for loops of Lazy Daisy stitches with disappearing ink marking pen or ball-head sewing pins, if desired. Remove each pin as stitch is made.

LARGE SAND DOLLAR

Make a magic ring, ch 1.

Rnd 1: 6 sc in ring, pull ring closed tight (6 sts).

Rnd 2: 2 sc in each st around. Place marker for beginning of rnd and move marker up as each rnd is completed (12 sts).

Rnd 3: *sc in next st, 2 sc in next st* 6 times (18 sts).

Rnd 4: *sc in next 2 sts, 2 sc in next st* 6 times (24 sts).

Rnd 5: sc in each st around.

Rnd 6: *sc in next 2 sts, sc2tog* 6 times (18 sts).

Rnd 7: *sc in next st, sc2tog* 6 times (12 sts).

Rnd 8: sc2tog 6 times (6 sts).

Fasten off with extra long tail. To close hole, thread tail in yarn needle, insert needle thru front loop of each st around opening & pull tight. Sew tail up thru center of Rnd 8 and out at center of Rnd 1. Embroider surface of sand dollar with 5 Lazy Daisy stitches as pictured. Be sure to keep back side of embroidery sts hidden between layers of sand dollar. Hide remaining tail inside. ♥

LAZY DAISY STITCH

1. Bring needle up at **A** and down at **B** leaving a loose loop of yarn.

2. Bring needle up at **C** and down at **D** making a small stitch to hold the loop in place.

Sand Castle

The "keep" is the center room of a castle. In this pattern, the keep is surrounded by 4 towers.

SUPPLIES

MEDIUM 4

H8/5mm crochet hook

200 yds of Worsted weight yarn in tan

Small piece of thin cardboard (cereal box weight)

Polyester fiberfill stuffing

Hot glue (optional)

6-inch craft or upholstery needle (optional)

KEEP

The keep is crocheted as a cube shape.

Note: crochet the keep in **front loops only** unless otherwise indicated.

For **top** of cube, make a magic ring, ch 1.

Rnd 1: 4 sc in ring, pull ring closed tight (4 sts).

Rnd 2: 3 sc in each st around. Place marker for beginning of rnd and move marker up as each rnd is completed (12 sts).

Rnd 3: sc in next st, *3 sc in next st, sc in next 2 sts* 3 times, 3 sc in next st, sc in next st (20 sts).

Rnd 4: sc in next 2 sts, *3 sc in next st, sc in next 4 sts* 3 times, 3 sc in next st, sc in next 2 sts (28 sts).

Rnd 5: sc in next 3 sts *3 sc in next st, sc in next 6 sts* 3 times, 3 sc in next st, sc in next 3 sts (36 sts).

Rnd 6: sc in next 4 sts, *3 sc in next st, sc in next 8 sts* 3 times, 3 sc in next st, sc in next 4 sts (44 sts).

For **sides** of cube,

Rnd 7: working in **back loops only**, sc in each st around (44 sts).

Rnds 8-18: resuming work in **front loops only**, sc in each st around.

Start to stuff and continue stuffing after each rnd.

For **bottom** of cube,

Rnd 19: working in **back loops only**, sc in each st around (44 sts).

Note: In the following rnds, **sc3tog** as follows: insert hook in st, yo, pull up a loop (2 loops on hook). Repeat 2 more times (4 loops on hook). Yo, pull thru all 4 loops on hook.

Rnd 20: resuming work in **front loops only**, sc in next 4 sts, *sc3tog, sc in next 8 sts* 3 times, sc3tog, sc in next 4 sts (36 sts).

Rnd 21: sc in next 3 sts, *sc3tog, sc in next 6 sts* 3 times, sc3tog, sc in next 3 sts (28 sts).

Rnd 22: sc in next 2 sts, *sc3tog, sc in next 4 sts* 3 times, sc3tog, sc in next 2 sts (20 sts).

Rnd 23: sc in next st, *sc3tog, sc in next 2 sts* 3 times, sc3tog, sc in next st (12 sts).

Rnd 24: sc3tog 4 times (4 sts).

Fasten off with extra long tail. Push final bits of stuffing thru ending hole. I like to use long tweezers for this (see page 11). As you stuff, push, squeeze and smooth the cube into shape. To close hole, thread ending tail onto needle, insert needle thru front loop of each stitch around opening and pull tight. Finish shaping cube as follows: Stab needle down thru center of Rnd 24 and out opposite side thru center of Rnd 1. Sew back into cube a bit off-center and out at opposite side. Pull gently on yarn tail to compress cube and create a flat top and bottom. Sew thru sides in this manner to refine the shape, if needed. Hide tail inside.

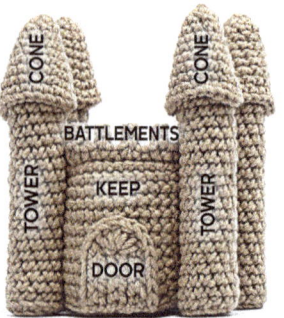

PARTS OF THE CASTLE

For **battlements** (notched edge),

Join in an unworked front loop of Rnd 7.

Rnd 25: *ch 5, sc in 1st ch made, sc in next 3 sts* around.

Fasten off. Weave in ends.

CONES (MAKE 4)

Make a magic ring, ch 1.

Rnd 1: 6 sc in ring, pull ring closed tight (6 sts).

Rnd 2: *sc in next 2 sts, 2 sc in next st* twice (8 sts).

Rnd 3: *sc in next 3 sts, 2 sc in next st* twice (10 sts).

Rnd 4: *sc in next 4 sts, 2 sc in next st* twice (12 sts).

Rnd 5: *sc in next 5 sts, 2 sc in next st* twice (14 sts).

Rnd 6: *sc in next 6 sts, 2 sc in next st* twice (16 sts).

Rnd 7: *sc in next 7 sts, 2 sc in next st* twice (18 sts).

Rnd 8: *sc in next 8 sts, 2 sc in next st* twice (20 sts).

Rnd 9: *sc in next 9 sts, 2 sc in next st* twice (22 sts).

Sl st in next st. Fasten off.

TOWERS (MAKE 4)

Note: A running stitch marker is ideal when crocheting these cylinders. See page 91.

Make a magic ring, ch 1.

Rnd 1: 6 sc in ring, pull ring closed tight (6 sts).

Rnd 2: 2 sc in each st around. Place marker for beginning of rnd and move marker up as each rnd is completed (12 sts).

Rnd 3: working in **back loops only**, sc in each st around.

Rnds 4-8: resuming work in **both loops**, sc in each st around.

For **base**, cut a 1-inch circle of thin cardboard by tracing a U.S. quarter or the template provided. Insert in bottom of cylinder to keep it flat. Start to stuff and continue stuffing as you work.

Tower Base Template

Rnds 9-22: sc in each st around.

Fasten off. Finish stuffing.

Stuff tip of cone, align edge with groove between Rnds 20-21 of tower and sew in place.

DOOR

Note: A chain 1 at the beginning of a row is for turning your work and does not count as a stitch.

Ch 6.

Row 1: starting in 2nd ch from hook, sc in each ch across (5 sts).

Rows 2-6: ch 1, turn, sc in each st across (5 sts).

Row 7: for **scallop**, do not turn, working forward across end of rows, sc in first st, skip next st, 6 dc in middle st, skip next st; referring to photo at right, **sl st in next 5 sts** (1 scallop, 5 sts).

Fasten off.

Dots = 5 slip sts

FINISHING

Attach door to front of keep with glue or sewing.

Attach towers to corners of keep with glue or sewing:

To **glue**, run a line of hot glue along corners of keep and press towers in place.

To **sew**, I like to hold the towers in place with thin bamboo skewers, then sew them in place using a 6-inch craft needle. With this long needle, I can sew through 1 tower, the keep and the next tower in 1 stitch.

Weave in ends. ♥

Beach Bag

The beach bag is crocheted in continuous rounds with **2 strands of yarn held together**. The multiple strands create a thick bag that holds its shape. If you've never crocheted with multiple strands, just pretend you are working with a single strand and make each stitch as if you were holding 1 strand of yarn.

SUPPLIES

H8/5mm and J10/6mm crochet hooks

125 yds of Worsted weight yarn in yellow

Small amount of Worsted weight yarn in gray

Small piece of cardboard

Small piece of wrapping paper or scrapbooking paper

Glue stick

MEDIUM 4

BAG

With J10/6mm hook and **2 strands** of yellow yarn held together, make a magic ring, ch 1.

Rnd 1: 4 sc in ring, pull ring closed tight (4 sts).

Rnd 2: 3 sc in each st around. Place marker for beginning of rnd and move marker up as each rnd is completed (12 sts).

Rnd 3: sc in next st, *3 sc in next st, sc in next 2 sts* 3 times, 3 sc in next st, sc in next st (20 sts).

Rnd 4: sc in next 2 sts, *3 sc in next st, sc in next 4 sts* 3 times, 3 sc in next st, sc in next 2 sts (28 sts).

Rnd 5: sc in next 3 sts, *3 sc in next st, sc in next 6 sts* 3 times, 3 sc in next st, sc in next 3 sts (36 sts).

Rnd 6: sc in next 4 sts, *3 sc in next st, sc in next 8 sts* 3 times, 3 sc in next st, sc in next 4 sts (44 sts).

Rnd 7: sc in next 5 sts, *3 sc in next st, sc in next 10 sts* 3 times, 3 sc in next st, sc in next 5 sts (52 sts).

Rnd 8: working in **back loops only**, sc in each st around.

Rnds 9-18: resuming work in **both loops**, sc in each st around; change to **2 strands** of gray yarn in last st of Rnd 18.

Rnd 19: sc in each st around.

Sl st in next st. Fasten off. Weave in ends.

HANDLES (MAKE 2)

With H8/5mm hook and a single strand of gray yarn, ch 65.

Rows 1-2: ch 1, turn, sc in each st across (65 sts).

Fasten off.

FINISHING

Cut a piece of cardboard 4" x 4". Clip off the pointy corners with tiny cuts to prevent them from poking thru the crocheted fabric. Glue decorative wrapping paper or scrapbooking paper to one side. Insert face up in bottom of bag.

Position handles on each side of bag as shown in picture and sew in place by sewing from bottom of bag to groove between Rnds 18-19. ♥

Peanut Butter & Jelly Sandwich

The sandwich is made with Worsted weight yarn in layers that are glued together. I have used red yarn for strawberry jelly, but purple and blue are also fun for grape and blueberry. Pack sandwiches in a snack-size plastic zipper bag for the beach party.

SUPPLIES

F5/3.75mm crochet hook

Small amount of Worsted weight yarn in beige, brown, gold & red

Hot glue

BREAD (MAKE 2)

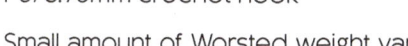

With beige yarn, make a magic ring, ch 1.

Rnd 1: 4 sc in ring, pull ring closed tight (4 sts).

Rnd 2: working in **front loops only**, 3 sc in each st around. Place marker for beginning of rnd and move marker up as each rnd is completed (12 sts).

Rnd 3: working in **front loops only**, sc in next st, 3 sc in next st, *sc in next 2 sts, 3 sc in next st* 3 times, sc in next st (20 sts).

Rnd 4: working in **front loops only**, sc in next 2 sts, 3 sc in next st, *sc in next 4 sts, 3 sc in next st* 3 times, sc in next 2 sts (28 sts).

Rnd 5: working in **back loops only,** change to brown yarn with sl st in next st, **sl st** in each remaining st around. Fasten off. To smooth the edge, sew brown ending tail down thru center of next brown st. Weave in end. Trim all tails to 1/2".

PEANUT BUTTER

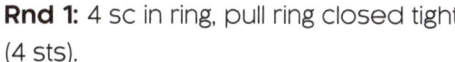

With gold yarn, make a magic ring, ch 1.

Rnd 1: 4 sc in ring, pull ring closed tight (4 sts).

Rnd 2: 3 sc in each st around. Place marker for beginning of rnd and move marker up as each rnd is completed (12 sts).

Rnd 3: sc in next st, 3 sc in next st, *sc in next 2 sts, 3 sc in next st* 3 times, sc in next st (20 sts).

Rnd 4: sc in next 2 sts, 3 sc in next st, *sc in next 4 sts, 3 sc in next st* 3 times, sc in next 2 sts (28 sts).

Sl st in next st. Fasten off. Weave in end. Trim tails to 1/2".

JELLY

With red yarn, make a magic ring, ch 1.

Rnd 1: 4 sc in ring, pull ring closed tight (4 sts).

Rnd 2: 3 sc in each st around. Place marker for beginning of rnd and move marker up as each rnd is completed (12 sts).

Rnd 3: sc in next st, 3 sc in next st, *sc in next 2 sts, 3 sc in next st* 3 times, sc in next st (20 sts).

Rnd 4: sc in next 2 sts, 3 sc in next st, *sc in next 4 sts, 3 sc in next st* 3 times, sc in next 2 sts (28 sts).

Sl st in next st. Fasten off. Weave in end. Trim tails to 1/2".

FINISHING

Stack jelly and peanut butter between bread and glue layers together. ♥

Pack sandwiches in a snack-size plastic zipper bag.

Bottled Water

SUPPLIES

F5/3.75mm crochet hook

Small amount of DK, Light Worsted yarn in blue and green

Small piece of thin cardboard (cereal box weight)

With blue yarn, make a magic ring, ch 1.

Rnd 1: 6 sc in ring, pull ring closed tight (6 sts).

Rnd 2: 2 sc in each st around. Place marker for beginning of rnd and move marker up as each rnd is completed (12 sts).

Rnd 3: *sc in next st, 2 sc in next st* 6 times (18 sts).

Rnd 4: working in **back loops only**, sc in each st around.

Rnds 5-9: resuming work in **both loops**, sc in each st around; change to green yarn in last st of Rnd 9.

For **base**, cut a 1-inch circle of thin cardboard by tracing a U.S. quarter or the template provided. Insert in bottle bottom. This will keep bottom flat and enable bottle to stand on its own.

Bottle Base Template

Rnd 10-15: sc in each st around; change to blue yarn in last st of Rnd 15.

Rnds 16-19: sc in each st around.

Stuff bottle and continue stuffing as you work.

Rnd 20: *sc in next st, sc2tog* 6 times (12 sts).

Rnd 21: *sc in next st, sc2tog* 4 times (8 sts).

Rnds 22-23: sc in each st around; change to green yarn in last st of Rnd 23.

Rnds 24-25: for **bottle cap**, sc in each st around.

Fasten off.

FINISHING

Finish stuffing bottle. Thread ending tail onto needle, insert needle thru **back loop** of each stitch around opening and pull tight to close hole. Shape bottle cap as follows: Stab needle down thru center of Rnd 25 and out thru center of green stripe. Sew back into bottle inserting needle close to point of exit and out thru bottle top. Pull gently on yarn tail to compress top and create a flat bottle cap. Sew up and down again in this manner as needed to get a nice flat cap. Hide yarn tail inside. ♥

Tortilla Chips

Little chips are made by working in rows. A bag is worked in the round from the top down. Ultra thin double-sided Velcro is used for the closure on the bag. This makes a fun noise when the bag is opened.

SUPPLIES

F5/3.75mm crochet hook

Small amount of DK, Light Worsted yarn in purple, blue & yellow

4" piece of ultra thin double sided hook-and-loop fastener tape (Velcro) in purple, 3/8" wide

Sewing thread

Fabric glue (optional)

Note: A chain 1 at the beginning of a round or row is for turning your work and does not count as a stitch.

TORTILLA CHIPS (MAKE 9)

Ch 2 with yellow yarn.

Row 1: 2 sc in second ch from hook (2 sts).

Row 2: ch 1, turn, sc in next st, 2 sc in last st (3 sts).

Row 3: ch 1, turn, sc in next 2 sts, 2 sc in last st (4 sts).

Row 4: ch 1, turn, sc in next 3 sts, 2 sc in last st (5 sts).

Row 5: ch 1, turn, sc in next 4 sts, 2 sc in last st (6 sts).

Row 6: ch 1, turn, sc in next 5 sts, 2 sc in last st (7 sts).

Row 7: ch 1, turn, sc in next 6 sts, 2 sc in last st (8 sts).

Fasten off. Weave in ends.

BAG

Ch 32 with purple yarn, join with sl st to first ch to make a ring using care not to twist the chain.

Rnd 1: sc in each ch around. Place marker for beginning of rnd and move marker up as each rnd is completed (32 sts).

Rnds 2-3: ch 1, **turn**, sc in each st around, join with sl st to first st (32 sts).

Rnds 4-9: sc in each st around; change to blue yarn in last st.

Rnd 10-13: sc in each st around.

Rnd 14: sc in each st around; change to purple yarn in last st.

Rnds 15-22: sc in each st around.

Fasten off. Flatten bag so that jogs in stripes from color changes are at a side crease. This will make them less noticeable.

Row 23: to **close bottom**, join purple yarn with sc at corner of bag, sc through all layers across (16 sts).

Row 24: ch 1, turn, sc in each st across.

Fasten off. Weave in ends.

FINISHING

Cut two 2" pieces of Velcro. Place one hook-side up, the other loop-side up, and sew to inside of bag along top edges.

Attach 1 chip to front of bag with glue or sewing thread. ♥

Ice Cream Cone

A highlight of a beach party is a stop at the ice cream stand!

SUPPLIES

F5/3.75mm crochet hook

Worsted weight yarn in tan & pink

Polyester fiberfill stuffing

ICE CREAM

With pink yarn, make a magic ring, ch 1.

Rnd 1: 8 sc in ring, pull ring closed tight (8 sts).

Rnd 2: 2 sc in each st around. Place marker for beginning of rnd and move marker up as each rnd is completed (16 sts).

Rnd 3: *sc in next st, 2 sc in next st* 8 times (24 sts).

Rnds 4-6: sc in each st around.

Rnd 7: *sc in next st, sc2tog* 8 times (16 sts).

Rnd 8: for **scallops**, working in **front loops only**, *(sc, hdc, sc) in next st, sl st in next st* 8 times (8 scallops).

Fasten off. Weave in end.

CONE

With tan yarn, make a magic ring, ch 1.

Rnd 1: 4 sc in ring, pull ring closed tight (4 sts).

Rnd 2: *sc in next st, 2 sc in next st* twice (6 sts).

Rnd 3: *sc in next 2 sts, 2 sc in next st* twice. Place marker for beginning of rnd and move marker up as each rnd is completed (8 sts).

Rnd 4: sc in each st around.

Rnd 5: *sc in next st, 2 sc in next st* 4 times (12 sts).

Rnd 6: sc in each st around.

Rnd 7: *sc in next 2 sts, 2 sc in next st* 4 times (16 sts).

Rnd 8: sc in each st around.

Sl st in next st. Fasten off with long tail.

FINISHING

Thead tail of cone in yarn needle. Place cone against ice cream as pictured. Working stitch-for-stitch, sew under **unworked back loops** of ice cream and **both loops** of cone, pausing when a small gap remains to insert stuffing. Hide tail inside. ♥

Orange Slice

The orange slice is stuffed with yarn tails only.

SUPPLIES

F5/3.75mm crochet hook

Small amount of DK, Light Worsted yarn in orange & white

With orange yarn, make a magic ring, ch 1.

Rnd 1: 6 sc in ring, pull ring closed tight (6 sts).

Rnd 2: 2 sc in each st around. Place marker for beginning of rnd and move marker up as each rnd is completed (12 sts).

Rnd 3: *sc in next st, 2 sc in next st* 6 times (18 sts).

Rnd 4: *sc in next 2 sts, 2 sc in next st* 6 times; change to white yarn in last st (24 sts).

Rnd 5: *sc in next 3 sts, 2 sc in next st* 6 times; change to orange yarn in last st (30 sts).

Rnd 6: *sc in next 4 sts, 2 sc in next st* 6 times (36 sts).

Pause to embroider segments: With white yarn, make 6 long stitches from center of Rnd 1 to edge of Rnd 5 (see Fig. A). Fold circle in half with back sides facing and stuff yarn tails inside.

Figure A

Figure B

Rnd 7: ch 1, working thru **both layers**, sl st in each st along edge to close up the orange slice. See Fig. B.

Fasten off. Hide yarn tail inside. ♥

Paper Plate

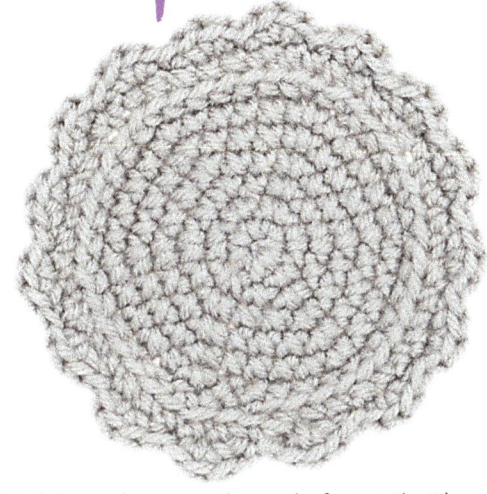

For rigid plates, choose a brand of yarn that is rather stiff. The plate begins with continuous rounds and changes to joined rounds at Rnd 6. Pile the plates with sandwiches, chips and orange slices for snacks at the beach party.

SUPPLIES

G6/4mm crochet hook

Small amount of Worsted weight yarn in white

Note: A chain 1 at the beginning of a round does not count as a stitch.

Make a magic ring, ch 1.

Rnd 1: 6 sc in ring, pull ring closed tight (6 sts).

Rnd 2: 2 sc in each st around. Place marker for beginning of rnd and move marker up as each rnd is completed (12 sts).

Rnd 3: *sc in next st, 2 sc in next st* 6 times (18 sts).

Rnd 4: *sc in next 2 sts, 2 sc in next st* 6 times (24 sts).

Rnd 5: *sc in next 3 sts, 2 sc in next st* 6 times (30 sts).

Rnd 6: *sc in next 4 sts, 2 sc in next st* 6 times, **join with sl st to first st** (36 sts).

Rnd 7: ch 1, working in **front loops only**, *sc in next 5 sts, 2 sc in next st* 6 times, **join with sl st to first st** (42 sts).

Rnd 8: ch 1, working in **back loops only**, *sc in next 6 sts, 2 sc in next st* 6 times, **join with sl st to first st** (48 sts).

Rnd 9: ch 1, resuming work in **both loops**, *3 sc in next st, skip next st, sl st in next st* around (16 scallops).

Fasten off. Weave in ends. ♥

Ray the Stingray

The round stingray with a pointed snout is common in the coastal waters of Southern California.

Note: A chain 1 at the beginning of a row is for turning your work and does not count as a stitch.

SIZE
4" diameter

SUPPLIES
G6/4mm crochet hook

Small amount of Worsted weight yarn in purple and white

2 black safety eyes, 7mm

Polyester fiberfill stuffing

TOP

With purple yarn, make a magic ring, ch 1.

Rnd 1: 6 sc in ring, pull ring closed tight (6 sts).

Rnd 2: 2 sc in each st around. Place marker for beginning of rnd and move marker up as each rnd is completed (12 sts).

Rnd 3: *sc in next st, 2 sc in next st* 6 times (18 sts).

Rnd 4: *sc in next 2 sts, 2 sc in next st* 6 times (24 sts).

Rnd 5: *sc in next 3 sts, 2 sc in next st* 6 times (30 sts).

Rnd 6: *sc in next 4 sts, 2 sc in next st* 6 times (36 sts).

Rnd 7: *sc in next 5 sts, 2 sc in next st* 6 times (42 sts).

Rnd 8: *sc in next 6 sts, 2 sc in next st* 6 times (48 sts).

Fasten off.

For **fin**, join in Stitch 45 of Rnd 8.

Row 9: dc in same st as where you joined, hdc in next st, sc in next st, sl st in next 2 sts, sc in next st, hdc in next st, dc in next st (8 sts).

Row 10: ch 1, turn, 2 sc in first st, sc in next 6 sts, 2 sc in last st (10 sts).

Row 11: ch 1, turn, 2 sc in first st, sc in next 8 sts, 2 sc in last st (12 sts).

Fasten off.

BOTTOM

With white yarn, make the same as top.

FINISHING

Attach **eyes** in top in groove between Rnds 6-7 with an interspace of 5 sts.

Place top and bottom together with back sides facing. Working thru both layers, join purple yarn, sc around perimeter making 3 sts in same st at tips of fin and pausing to stuff when nearly done: stuff along center from nose to fin leaving sides unstuffed. Fasten off.

For **tail**, join purple yarn 1 stitch from center of fin, ch 11, turn, sc in 2nd ch from hook and in each remaining ch across (10 sts).

Sl st in next st of fin. Fasten off. Weave in ends. ♥

Clawde the Crab

SIZE 3 1/2" diameter (body); 5 1/2" diameter (including legs)

SUPPLIES

G6/4mm crochet hook

Small amount of Worsted weight yarn in red

2 black safety eyes, 7mm

Polyester fiberfill stuffing

BODY (MAKE 2)

Make a magic ring, ch 1.

Rnd 1: 6 sc in ring, pull ring closed tight (6 sts).

Rnd 2: 2 sc in each st around. Place marker for beginning of rnd and move marker up as each rnd is completed (12 sts).

Rnd 3: *sc in next st, 2 sc in next st* 6 times (18 sts).

Rnd 4: *sc in next 2 sts, 2 sc in next st* 6 times (24 sts).

Rnd 5: *sc in next 3 sts, 2 sc in next st* 6 times (30 sts).

Rnd 6: *sc in next 4 sts, 2 sc in next st* 6 times (36 sts).

Rnd 7: *sc in next 5 sts, 2 sc in next st* 6 times (42 sts).

Sl st in next st. Fasten off.

CLAWS (MAKE 2)

Make a magic ring, ch 1.

Rnd 1: 4 sc in ring, pull ring closed tight (4 sts).

Rnd 2: *sc in next st, 2 sc in next st* 2 times. Place marker for beginning of rnd and move marker up as each rnd is completed (6 sts).

Rnd 3: 2 sc in each st around (12 sts).

Rnds 4-6: sc in each st around.

Rnd 7: *sc in next 2 sts, sc2tog* 3 times (9 sts).

Rnd 8: *sc in next st, sc2tog* 3 times (6 sts).

Rnds 9-10: sc in each st around.

Sl st in next st. Fasten off.

Stuff lightly. Pinch tip into a point.

LEGS (MAKE 6)

Make a magic ring, ch 1.

Rnd 1: 6 sc in ring, pull ring closed tight (6 sts).

Rnds 2-6: sc in each st around.

Sl st in next st. Fasten off.

Do not stuff.

FINISHING

Attach **eyes** to body top in groove between Rnds 5-6 with an interspace of 4 sts.

Place body pieces together with back sides facing. Working thru both layers, join new yarn and sc around perimeter — pausing to stuff lightly when gap is nearly closed. Fasten off.

Sew claws and legs to body as pictured. ♥

Seabert the Seagull

SIZE 4" tall

SUPPLIES

G6/4mm crochet hook

Small amount of Worsted weight yarn in white, gray, yellow and black

2 black safety eyes, 7mm

Glue (for eyes, see page 11), optional

Polyester fiberfill stuffing

HEAD & BODY

With white yarn, make a magic ring, ch 1.

Rnd 1: 5 sc in ring, pull ring closed tight (5 sts).

Rnd 2: 2 sc in each st around. Place marker for beginning of rnd and move marker up as each rnd is completed (10 sts).

Rnd 3: *sc in next st, 2 sc in next st* 5 times (15 sts).

Rnd 4: *sc in next 2 sts, 2 sc in next st* 5 times (20 sts).

Rnds 5-10: sc in each st around.

Attach **eyes** between Rnds 7-8 with an interspace of 5 sts.

If preferred, these can be attached with glue after final assembly.

Rnd 11: *sc in next 4 sts, 2 sc in next st* 4 times (24 sts).

Rnd 12: *sc in next 3 sts, 2 sc in next st* 6 times (30 sts).

Rnds 13-18: sc in each st around.

Rnd 19: *sc in next 3 sts, sc2tog* 6 times (24 sts).

Rnd 20: *sc in next 2 sts, sc2tog* 6 times (18 sts).

Rnd 21: *sc in next st, sc2tog* 6 times (12 sts).

Pause to stuff. Shape and squeeze as you stuff to define head from body.

Rnd 22: sc2tog 6 times (6 sts).

Fasten off. Finish adding stuffing while keeping the bottom flat. Thread ending tail onto needle, insert needle thru front loop of each stitch around opening and pull tight to close hole. Hide yarn tail inside.

WINGS (MAKE 2)

With gray yarn, make a magic ring, ch 1.

Rnd 1: 6 sc in ring, pull ring closed tight (6 sts).

Rnd 2: 2 sc in each st around. Place marker for beginning of rnd and move marker up as each rnd is completed (12 sts).

Rnds 3-6: sc in each st around.

Rnd 7: sc2tog twice, sc in next 8 sts (10 sts).

Rnd 8: sc2tog twice, sc in next 6 sts (8 sts).

Rnd 9: sc2tog twice, sc in next 4 sts (6 sts).

Fasten off. Do not stuff. Thread ending tail onto needle, insert needle thru front loop of each stitch around opening and pull tight to close hole. Flatten with decreases along lower edge of wing. Sew yarn tail thru inside of wing emerging at groove between Rnds 3-4 to be used for sewing wing to body.

LEGS & FEET (MAKE 2)

With yellow yarn, ch 6.

Starting in 2nd ch from hook, sl st in next 2 chs, ch 3; starting in 2nd ch from hook, sl st in next 2 chs, ch 3; starting in 2nd ch from hook, sl st in next 2 chs; sc in next 3 sts along starting chain. Fasten off.

BEAK

With yellow yarn, make a magic ring, ch 1.

Rnd 1: 5 sc in ring, pull ring closed tight (5 sts).

Rnd 2: 2 sc in first st, sc in next 4 sts (6 sts).

Fasten off. Push handle of crochet hook into center of Rnd 1 to pop beak into shape.

Row 4: crocheting thru both layers, **sl st** in each st across (6 sts).

Fasten off. Weave in end.

TAIL

With black yarn, ch 12, join with sl st to 1st ch to make a ring using care not to twist the chain.

Rnds 1-3: sc in each st around. Place marker for beginning of rnd and move marker up as each rnd is completed.

Flatten piece with working yarn at right corner.

FINISHING

Sew tail to Rnd 19 of body.

Sew legs to bottom of body with feet sticking out at front.

Pin wings to sides of body with wing tops at groove between Rnds 9-10. Sew in place with a few sts behind top of wing.

Sew beak in place as pictured. ♥

Starla the Starfish

Starla begins with the creation of 5 small cones. These are connected to form the arms. Next, the front and back of the starfish are filled in by working in rounds.

SIZE 5" diameter

SUPPLIES

G6/4mm crochet hook
50 yds of Worsted weight yarn in pink
Small amount of Worsted weight yarn in black
2 black safety eyes, 7mm
15 small white beads, sequins or buttons
Sewing thread
Polyester fiberfill stuffing
Glue (for eyes or embellishments, see page 11), optional

ARMS (MAKE 5)

Be sure to keep piece turned right-side out as you work.

Make a magic ring, ch 1.

Rnd 1: 4 sc in ring, pull ring closed tight (4 sts).

Rnd 2: *sc in next st, 2 sc in next st* twice. Place marker for beginning of rnd and move marker up as each rnd is completed (6 sts).

Rnd 3: *sc in next 2 sts, 2 sc in next st* twice (8 sts).

Rnd 4: *sc in next 3 sts, 2 sc in next st* twice (10 sts).

Rnd 5: *sc in next 4 sts, 2 sc in next st* twice (12 sts).

Rnd 6: *sc in next 5 sts, 2 sc in next st* twice (14 sts).

Rnd 7: *sc in next 6 sts, 2 sc in next st* twice (16 sts).

Rnd 8: sc in each st around.

Sl st in next st. Fasten off with long tail. Tuck tails inside to be used later.

MARKING THE ARMS

When the starfish is assembled, 4 sts on each arm are left unworked. By marking the sts to be skipped, it's easy to identify them.

Cut 10 pieces of contrasting yarn to use as markers.

On each arm, locate the final sl st. Counting clockwise from the sl st, hook a marker thru Sts 7-8 and Sts 15-16 (see Fig. A).

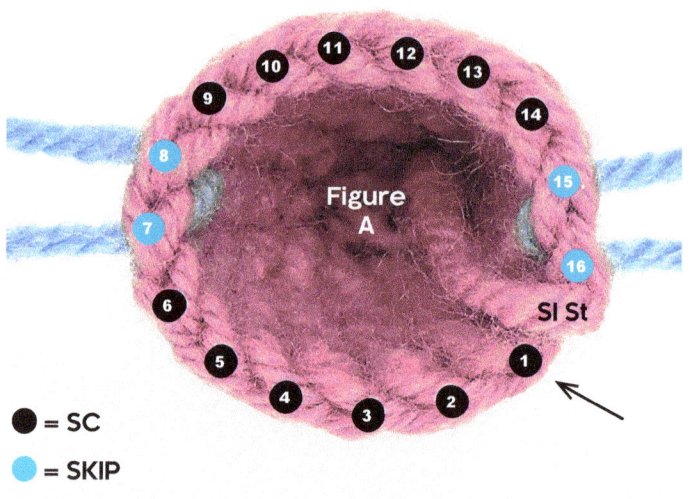

STARFISH FRONT

To connect arms for starfish front, work in Sts 1-6 of each arm (see Fig. A).

Rnd 1: take any arm, join with sc in first st (see arrow, Fig. A), sc in next 5 sts. Repeat with remaining arms (30 sts).

The assembly will now look like Fig. B.

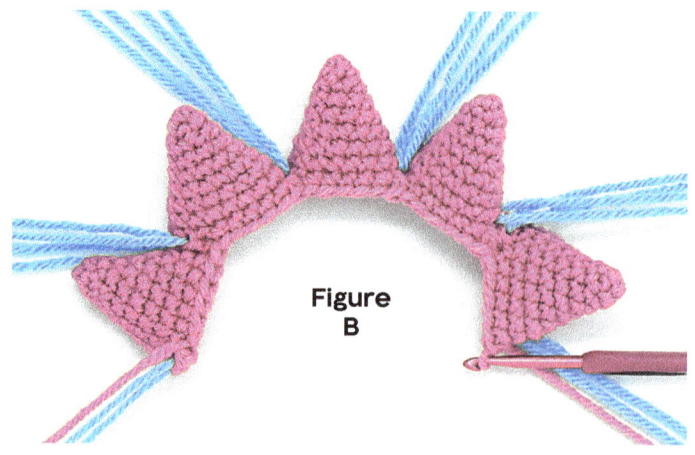

Start Rnd 2 in first st of next arm (see Fig. C).

STARFISH BACK

To connect the arms for starfish back, work in Sts 9-14 (see Fig. A) of each arm.

As you work Rnd 1, be sure to skip over the sts that are marked with contrasting yarn.

Rnd 1: starting with any arm, join with sc in first st (see arrow, Fig. F), sc in each st around. Place marker for beginning of rnd and move marker up as each rnd is completed (30 sts).

Rnd 2: *sc in next 4 sts, sc2tog* 5 times. Place marker for beginning of rnd and move marker up as each rnd is completed (25 sts).

Rnd 3: *sc in next 3 sts, sc2tog* 5 times (20 sts).

Rnd 4: *sc in next 2 sts, sc2tog* 5 times (15 sts).

Rnd 5: *sc in next st, sc2tog* 5 times (10 sts).

Sl st in next st. Fasten off.

To close hole (see Fig. D), thread tail in yarn needle, insert needle thru front loop of each st around opening & pull tight. Secure with a knot on wrong side. Trim excess tail.

Rnd 2: *sc in next 4 sts, sc2tog* 5 times (25 sts).

Pause to close holes between arms: Remove marker-yarn. Pull out long tails tucked inside arms, use them to sew holes closed and secure each with a knot. Trim excess from tails.

Rnd 3: *sc in next 3 sts, sc2tog* 5 times (20 sts).

Rnd 4: *sc in next 2 sts, sc2tog* 5 times (15 sts).

Stuff the starfish.

Rnd 5: *sc in next st, sc2tog* 5 times (10 sts).

Sl st in next st. Fasten off. Finish adding stuffing.

To close hole, thread tail in yarn needle, insert needle thru front loop of each st around opening & pull tight. Secure tail inside starfish. Squeeze starfish into shape.

FINISHING

Embroider a simple **mouth** with black yarn: Bring needle out at A, insert at B leaving the yarn loose to form mouth. Secure shape with a dot of glue OR bring needle out again at C, go over loose strand and insert needle at D to make a tiny stitch. Secure ends inside.

Starfish front is done (see Fig. E). Attach **eyes** in groove between Rnds 3-4 with interspace of 5 sts or glue in place after final assembly.

Attach beads, sequins or buttons to front of arms with sewing or glue as pictured on page 82. ♥

Sandy the Dog

A black animal eye can be substituted for the triangle nose if desired. Sandy loves to play fetch with a tennis ball at the beach, so be sure to make Sandy's ball, too!

SIZE
4 1/2" tall

SUPPLIES

G6/4mm crochet hook

Small amount of Worsted weight yarn in tan fleck, brown fleck, black, green and yellow

2 black safety eyes, 7mm

Black triangle animal nose, 7mm

Polyester fiberfill stuffing

Glue (for eye & nose, see page 11), optional

Thin bamboo skewer (optional)

HEAD

With tan yarn, make a magic ring, ch 1.

Rnd 1: 6 sc in ring, pull ring closed almost tight (6 sts).

Rnd 2: 2 sc in each st around. Place marker for beginning of rnd and move marker up as each rnd is completed (12 sts).

Rnds 3-4: sc in each st around.

Rnd 5: *sc in next st, 2 sc in next st* 6 times (18 sts).

Rnd 6: *sc in next 2 sts, 2 sc in next st* 6 times (24 sts).

Rnd 7: *sc in next 3 sts, 2 sc in next st* 6 times (30 sts).

Rnds 8-11: sc in each st around.

Work on face. Next the nose and eyes are attached. (If preferred, these features can be attached with glue after final assembly.)

- **Nose:** with black yarn, embroider a stitch from center of Rnd 1 to groove between Rnds 2-3 as pictured. Attach nose at center of Rnd 1.

- **Eyes:** attach to head in groove between Rnds 6-7 with an interspace of 5-6 sts.

Rnd 12: *sc in next 3 sts, sc2tog* 6 times (24 sts).

Rnd 13: *sc in next 2 sts, sc2tog* 6 times (18 sts).

Rnd 14: *sc in next 4 sts, sc2tog* 3 times (15 sts).

Start to stuff head and continue stuffing after each rnd.

Rnd 15: *sc in next 3 sts, sc2tog* 3 times (12 sts).

Rnd 16: sc2tog 6 times (6 sts).

Fasten off.

Finish adding stuffing. To close hole, thread tail in yarn needle, insert needle thru front loop of each st around opening and pull tight. Weave in end. Squeeze head into shape.

BODY

With brown yarn, make a magic ring, ch 1.

Rnd 1: 6 sc in ring, pull ring closed tight (6 sts).

Rnd 2: 2 sc in each st around; change to tan yarn in last st. Place marker for beginning of rnd and move marker up as each rnd is completed (12 sts).

Rnd 3: *sc in next st, 2 sc in next st* 6 times (18 sts).

Rnds 4-15: sc in each st around.

Rnd 16: *sc in next st, sc2tog* 6 times (12 sts).

Pause to stuff.

Rnd 17: sc2tog 6 times (6 sts).

Fasten off. Finish adding stuffing. Thread ending tail onto needle, insert needle thru front loop of each stitch around opening and pull tight to close hole. Hide yarn tail inside.

EARS (MAKE 2)

With brown yarn, ch 10. Now work around the chain.

Row 1: sc in 2nd ch from hook, sc in next 7 chs, 3 sc in last ch, sc in next 8 chs.

Row 2: ch 1, turn, sc in next 8 sts, 2 sc in next 3 sts, sc in next 8 sts.

Fasten off.

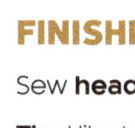

LEGS (MAKE 4)

With brown yarn, make a magic ring, ch 1.

Rnd 1: 6 sc in ring, pull ring closed tight (6 sts).

Rnd 2: 2 sc in each st around. Place marker for beginning of rnd and move marker up as each rnd is completed (12 sts).

Rnd 3: sc in each st around; join with sl st in first st and change to tan yarn in the sl st (12 sts).

Rnds 4-5: sc in each st around.

Rnd 6: *sc in next 2 sts, sc2tog* 3 times (9 sts).

Rnd 7: sc in each st around.

Sl st in next st. Fasten off.

Stuff Leg.

TAIL

With brown yarn, make a magic ring, ch 1.

Rnd 1: 4 sc in ring, pull ring closed tight (4 sts).

Rnd 2: *sc in next st, 2 sc in next st* 2 times (6 sts).

Rnds 3-?: sc in each st around until tail is about 1 1/2" long.

Sl st in next st. Fasten off.

FINISHING

Sew **head** to body as shown in picture.

Tip: I like to use a thin bamboo skewer (or knitting needle) to position the head and hold it in place as I sew. Just stab skewer thru head, then into body, and adjust until you get the look you like. This method can also be used to position the remaining appendages.

Sew **legs** to bottom of body. Sew **tail** in place.

Position front corners of **ears** on Rnd 9 of head and aligned with eyes. Sew in place. Glue top third of ears against head, if desired.

Collar: With green yarn, chain a string long enough to fit around dog's neck. Fasten off. Knot collar around neck. Hide yarn tails inside body.

SANDY'S BALL

With yellow yarn, make a magic ring, ch 1.

Rnd 1: 6 sc in ring, pull ring closed tight (6 sts).

Rnd 2: 2 sc in each st around. Place marker for beginning of rnd and move marker up as each rnd is completed (12 sts).

Rnd 3: *sc in next st, 2 sc in next st* 6 times (18 sts).

Rnds 4-6: sc in each st around.

Rnd 7: *sc in next st, sc2tog* 6 times (12 sts).

Rnd 8: sc2tog 6 times (6 sts).

Fasten off. Stuff ball. Thread ending tail onto needle, insert needle thru front loop of each stitch around opening and pull tight to close hole.

Weave in end. ♥

85

Tropical Fish Sleeping Bag

SUPPLIES

H8/5mm crochet hook

125 yds of Worsted weight yarn, self-striping

2 animal eyes, 24mm

Invisible sewing thread (optional)

Note: A chain 1 at the beginning of a row is for turning your work and does not count as a stitch.

HEAD AND BODY

Ch 24, join with sl st to 1st ch to make a ring using care not to twist the chain.

*In rnds 1-24, you will be increasing by 1 stitch at the end of **each round**.*

Rnds 1-24: sc in each st around until 1 st remains, 2 sc in last st. Place marker for beginning of rnd and move marker up as each rnd is completed (48 sts at Rnd 24).

Rnds 25-40: sc in each st around (48 sts).

*In rnds 41-43, you will be decreasing by 1 stitch at the end of **each round**.*

Rnds 41-43: sc in each st around until 2 sts remain, sc2tog (45 sts at Rnd 43).

Fasten off. Flatten piece so that ending yarn tail is at center back of fish. Sew bottom end closed.

TAIL

Ch 10.

Row 1: ch 1, turn, sc in each ch across (10 sts).

Work remaining rows in **back loops only.**

Row 2: ch 1, turn, sc in next 8 sts, sc2tog (9 sts).

Row 3: ch 1, turn, sc2tog, sc in next 7 sts (8 sts).

Row 4: ch 1, turn, sc in next 6 sts, sc2tog (7 sts).

Row 5: ch 1, turn, sc2tog, sc in next 5 sts (6 sts).

Row 6: ch 1, turn, sc in next 4 sts, sc2tog (5 sts).

Row 7: ch 1, turn, 2 sc in next st, sc in next 4 sts (6 sts).

Row 8: ch 1, turn, sc in next 5 sts, 2 sc in next st (7 sts).

Row 9: ch 1, turn, 2 sc in next st, sc in next 6 sts (8 sts).

Row 10: ch 1, turn, sc in next 7 sts, 2 sc in next st (9 sts).

Row 11: ch 1, turn, 2 sc in next st, sc in next 8 sts (10 sts).

Fasten off.

The Tropical Fish Sleeping Bag is made with self-striping yarn. This type of yarn creates stripes as you crochet without the need to change colors. See page 95 for the specific yarn used here.

The head and body section of the sleeping bag is worked in rounds from the bottom up. A running stitch marker is ideal here (see page 91). The tail and fins are crocheted in rows using the back loops to create a ridged effect.

FINS (MAKE 2)

Ch 10.

Row 1: ch 1, turn, sc in each ch across (10 sts).

Work remaining rows in **back loops only.**

Row 2: ch 1, turn, sc in next 8 sts, sc2tog (9 sts).

Row 3: ch 1, turn, sc2tog, sc in next 7 sts (8 sts).

Row 4: ch 1, turn, sc in next 6 sts, sc2tog (7 sts).

Row 5: ch 1, turn, sc2tog, sc in next 5 sts (6 sts).

Row 6: ch 1, turn, sc in next 4 sts, sc2tog (5 sts).

Row 7: ch 1, turn, sc2tog, sc in next 3 sts (4 sts).

Row 8: ch 1, turn, sc in next 2 sts, sc2tog (3 sts).

Row 9: ch 1, turn, sc2tog, sc in next st (2 sts).

Row 10: ch 1, turn, sc2tog (1 st).

Fasten off.

FINISHING

With invisible sewing thread or yarn tails, sew tail and fins in place as shown in photos.

Weave in ends.

Attach eyes as pictured. ♥

GOOD NIGHT, SLEEP TIGHT!

Stitches

SLIP KNOT

This is used to make a starting loop on the crochet hook.

1. Make a loop about 5 inches from end of yarn. Insert hook in loop and hook onto supply yarn (yarn coming from ball) at A.

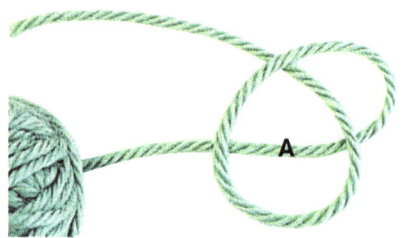

2. Pull yarn through loop.

3. Pull yarn ends to tighten loop around hook.

CHAIN (CH)

Start with a slip knot on hook.

1. Bring yarn **over** hook from back to front. Catch yarn with hook and pull it through the loop —

to look like this. One ch is done.

SLIP STITCH (SL ST)

1. Insert hook in stitch. Yarn over and pull through stitch and through loop on hook (A and B).

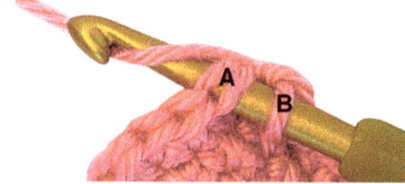

2. The sl st is done.

SINGLE CROCHET (SC)

This simple stitch is the primary stitch for amigurumi.

1. Insert hook in designated stitch. Note: Put hook under **both loops** that form v-shape at top of stitch unless otherwise instructed.

2. Yarn over and pull through the stitch (A).

You now have 2 loops on the hook:

3. Yarn over and pull through both loops on hook.

4. You now have 1 loop on hook and the sc stitch is done.

HALF DOUBLE CROCHET (HDC)

1. Yarn over and insert hook in designated stitch.

2. Yarn over and pull through the stitch (A).

You now have 3 loops on hook:

3. Yarn over and pull through all 3 loops on hook (A, B & C).

4. You now have 1 loop on hook and the hdc stitch is done.

DOUBLE CROCHET (DC)

1. Yarn over and insert hook in designated stitch.

2. Yarn over and pull through the stitch (A).

You now have 3 loops on hook:

3. Yarn over and pull through 1st 2 loops on hook (A and B).

You now have 2 loops on hook:

4. Yarn over and pull through both loops on hook.

5. You now have 1 loop on hook and the dc stitch is done.

INVISIBLE DECREASE (INVDEC)

This is a very neat way to decrease 2 stitches into 1 stitch.

1. Insert hook in **front loop** of first st. DO NOT YARN OVER. You now have 2 loops on hook.

2. Insert hook in **front loop** of next st. You now have 3 loops on hook.

3. Yarn over and pull through first 2 loops on hook. You now have 2 loops on hook.

4. Yarn over and pull through both loops on hook.

SINGLE CROCHET 2 TOGETHER DECREASE (SC2TOG)

This stitch is used to decrease 2 stitches into 1 stitch.

1. Insert hook in first stitch, yarn over and pull up a loop. You now have 2 loops on hook.

2. Insert hook in next stitch, yarn over and pull up a loop. You now have 3 loops on hook.

3. Yarn over and pull through all 3 loops on hook.

SINGLE CROCHET 3 TOGETHER DECREASE (SC3TOG)

This stitch is used to decrease 3 stitches into 1 stitch.

1. Insert hook in first stitch, yarn over and pull up a loop. You now have 2 loops on hook.

2. Insert hook in next stitch, yarn over and pull up a loop. You now have 3 loops on hook.

3. Insert hook in next stitch, yarn over and pull up a loop. You now have 4 loops on hook.

4. Yarn over and pull through all 4 loops on hook.

Techniques

★ MAGIC RING

Most of my amigurumi begins with the Magic Ring. This is an adjustable loop that makes a neat center when crocheting in the round. If you're not familiar with it, you may want to watch a YouTube tutorial. It's not difficult — and well worth it.

An alternative to the Magic Ring, if desired, is the Chain 2 Method. For this method, ch 2, then begin Rnd 1 by working the required number of sts as stated in the pattern into the 2nd ch from the hook. This method is easier for beginners and perfectly acceptable but will leave a small hole in the middle of the first round (see photos below).

Magic Ring   Chain 2 Method

Make the **Magic Ring** as follows:

1. Make a ring a few inches from end of yarn. Grasp ring between thumb and index finger where the join makes an X. Insert hook in ring, hook onto supply yarn at Y and pull up a loop —

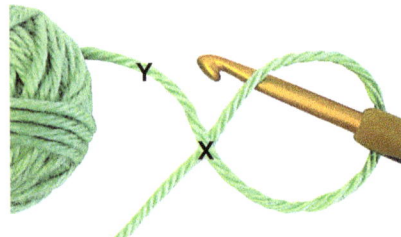

to look like this.

2. Chain 1 —

to look like this. This chain does not count as a stitch.

3. Insert hook into ring so you're crocheting over ring and yarn tail. Pull up a loop to begin your first Single Crochet —

and complete the Single Crochet.

4. Continue to crochet over ring and yarn tail for the specified number of Single Crochets for the 1st round.

5. Pull tail to close up ring. To begin the 2nd round, insert hook in 1st stitch of 1st round (see arrow).

BEGIN 2ND RND HERE

WORKING IN THE ROUND

Working in the round is crocheting in a continuous spiral. A lot of amigurumi is worked this way.

WORKING IN LOOPS

When a Single Crochet stitch is made, you will see 2 loops in a v-shape at the top of the stitch. To crochet the patterns in this book, insert your hook under **both loops** unless instructed otherwise. Crocheting in the "front loops only" or the "back loops only" is sometimes used for a different effect.

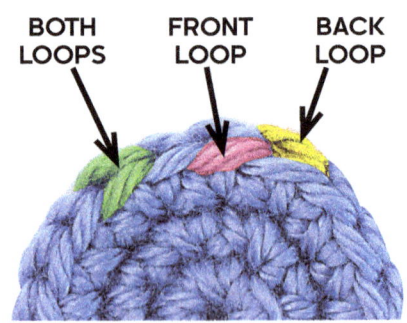

BOTH LOOPS FRONT LOOP BACK LOOP

CHANGING COLORS

To change color while single crocheting, work last stitch of old color to last yarn over, yarn over with new color and pull through both loops to complete the stitch.

ROTATING YOUR HOOK

When you wrap yarn over your hook, the front of the hook should be facing you. Then when it's time to pull the yarn through the loop on the hook, rotate the hook downward. It will slide easily through the loop instead of getting caught.

COUNTING ROUNDS

Periodically, it is good to count your rounds to ensure your place in a pattern. Fortunately, rounds are clearly defined and counting is easy. Each round makes a ridge. A groove separates the rounds. You only need to count the ridges. Take a look at the photo below to see that the circle has 5 rounds.

USING STITCH MARKERS

It can be tricky to keep track of your place when working in the round, so be sure to use a stitch marker. Place the stitch marker in the first stitch of a round — after completing the stitch. When you've crocheted all the way around, remove the stitch marker, make the next stitch, and replace the marker in the stitch just made. This will be the first stitch of the next round.

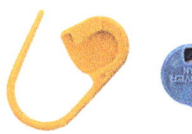 

RUNNING STITCH MARKER

Stitch markers are essential in amigurumi to mark specific spots on your work. You can use one any time you feel it is necessary and sometimes the pattern will indicate that a marker is needed. A Running Stitch Marker is a scrap of yarn in a contrasting color that is woven back and forth between rounds. I especially like this type of marker for narrow cylinders such as arms and legs.

When you complete your first round, lay your "marker-yarn" over your work before starting the next round. Then, when you work the first stitch of the next round, the yarn will be trapped between the stitches. At the end of each successive round, fold the marker-yarn back over your work: if it's in the back, fold it to the front, if it's in the front, fold it to the back. This way the yarn is flipped back and forth — between the last stitch of each round and the first stitch of the next round. When you're done, simply pull the marker-yarn out.

FASTENING OFF

This is the way to finish a piece so that it won't unravel. When you're done crocheting, cut the yarn and leave a tail. Wrap the tail over your hook and pull it all the way through the last loop left on your hook. Pull the tail tight and it will make a knot.

SMOOTHING THE EDGE

When fastening off, the knot can make a small bump in the edge of your work so that, for example, a round shape will not look as round as it should. To make the edge smooth, thread the long tail in a yarn needle and insert the needle down thru the center "V" of the next stitch.

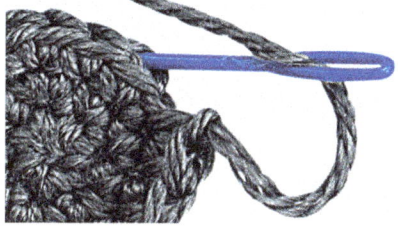

JOINING YARN

To join new yarn onto a crocheted item, such as to make a border, strap or sleeve, insert hook in desired stitch, make a loop and pull it through the stitch.

JOINING WITH SL ST

Start with a Slip Knot on hook. Insert hook in specified stitch. Yarn over and pull through the stitch and the loop on the hook.

JOINING WITH SC

Put yarn on hook with a Slip Knot. Insert hook in indicated stitch. Complete sc as shown in Single Crochet tutorial, page 88, steps 2-4

ASSEMBLING

The assembly stage of amigurumi is an exciting time. This is when various pieces are sewn together and the project blossoms in cuteness! Thread a yarn needle with the tail of your auxiliary piece (arm, leg, etc.) and use a whip stitch or running stitch to sew it in place. You may want to pin your pieces in place beforehand to be sure the position looks good. A sewing needle and thread can also be used to sew your parts together. In some cases, this will make the stitches less visible.

WEAVING IN ENDS

The assembly of every pattern includes the instruction to "weave in the ends". This is the way to hide and secure all of your straggly yarn tails. Follow this "Rule of 3": (1) Thread yarn tail into a yarn needle, skim thru back of sts on wrong side of work for a short distance; (2) turn and go in opposite direction thru different sts; (3) turn and go in original direction to lock the yarn in place. Trim end close. When you turn to the right side, you should not see the woven ends. They should be tucked into the middle of your crocheted fabric.

FRENCH KNOT

Bring needle up from wrong side at A. Place needle close to fabric and wrap yarn around needle 2 or 3 times. Push needle down at a point near A.

RUNNING STITCH

The Running Stitch is formed by a detached series of Straight Stitches. Make it by running the needle up and down the fabric at a regular distance. Come up at A, down at B, up at C, down at D, up at E, down at F, etc.

ADDING WIRE

Optional armatures, or wire frameworks, can make amigurumi more dynamic by enabling a character to hold a pose. It can be placed in the arms, legs or both.

PARTIAL ARMATURE

If your doll is made for display, this will make your doll more like an action figure than a cuddly stuffie. Use a heavy wire of 16 to 19 gauge. Begin when the doll's head/body are stuffed and connected, and all parts are made.

For the **arms**, stuff hands only. The arms won't need stuffed. Lay doll down with arms outstretched in position and cut a piece of wire to that length plus a bit extra (~1/2" to 1").

1. Bend one end into a small loop with needle-nose pliers and insert into first arm thru to hand.

2. Insert exposed end of wire into body where the arm will be placed.

3. Push wire all the way thru body to opposite side where you will sew the other arm.

4. Bend exposed tip of wire into a small loop and insert into 2nd arm.

5. Sew both arms to body around wire core.

For yarn-jointed **legs**, prepare a piece of wire the length of each leg with a small loop at each end. Insert wire in leg and stuff around it using long craft tweezers. Finish assembly according to pattern instructions. Note: When pushing needle thru top of leg for yarn-jointing (see page 16, Fig. X) be sure needle goes thru loop at top of wire.

Resources

YARN
Amazon
amazon.com

Herrschners
herrschners.com

Lovecrafts
lovecrafts.com

Michaels
michaels.com

NOTIONS
Amazon
amazon.com

Joann Fabric and Craft Stores
joann.com

SAFETY EYES
Amazon
amazon.com

Etsy
etsy.com

BEADS
Amazon
amazon.com

Etsy
etsy.com

Michaels
michaels.com

VIDEO TUTORIALS

youtube.com
Search on the name of the stitch or technique you want to learn.

pinterest.com/LindalooEnt/
Visit my Pinterest page to view video tutorials for the stitches and techniques used in this book. Look for the board named "Amigurumi Tutorials".

Yarn

The following yarns were used for these projects.

Summer (Worsted, #4)
Lion Brand "Vanna's Choice": Beige & Lemon

Sunny (Worsted, #4)
Lion Brand "Vanna's Choice": Beige & Mustard

Flamingo Bathing Suit (DK, Light Worsted, #3)
Stylecraft "Special DK": Lipstick, Fondant, Black & White

Anchor Swim Trunks (DK, Light Worsted, #3)
Stylecraft "Special DK": Mustard & Denim

2-Piece Bathing Suit (DK, Light Worsted, #3)
Stylecraft "Special DK": Cloud Blue & Fondant

Board Shorts (DK, Light Worsted, #3)
Stylecraft "Special DK": Shrimp, Graphite & Turquoise
Also pictured with:
Stylecraft "Special DK": Lipstick & Graphite
Bernat "Softee Baby": Soft Red
and
Stylecraft "Special DK": Lipstick, Saffron & Spice
and
Stylecraft "Special DK": Meadow, Citron & Spice
and
Stylecraft "Special DK": Lavender, Aster & Aspen
and
Stylecraft "Special DK": Mocha, Copper & Khaki

Beach Wrap (DK, Light Worsted, #3)
Ice Yarns "Magic Light": Self-Striping Purple, Pink, Blue, Yellow, Green

Beach Cover-Up (DK, Light Worsted, #3)
Stylecraft "Special DK": Turquoise, Spice, Sunshine & French Navy

Over-the Rainbow Sundress (DK, Light Worsted, #3)
Stylecraft "Special DK": Clementine, Pomegranate, Spice, Saffron, Grass Green, Turquoise & Violet

Under-the-Sea Sundress (DK, Light Worsted, #3)
    Stylecraft "Special DK": Lavender, Meadow & Fondant

Striped Sundress (DK, Light Worsted, #3)
    Stylecraft "Special DK": Fondant & Candyfloss

Starfish Sundress (DK, Light Worsted, #3)
    Stylecraft "Special DK": Citron & Meadow

Basic Shirt (DK, Light Worsted, #3)
    Stylecraft "Special DK": Citron

Crab Shirt (DK, Light Worsted, #3)
    Stylecraft "Special DK": Turquoise & Tomato

Sunshine Shirt (DK, Light Worsted, #3)
    Stylecraft "Special DK": Violet, Saffron & Spice

Palm Tree Shirt (DK, Light Worsted, #3)
    Stylecraft "Special DK": Fondant, Cypress & Walnut

Sailboat Shirt (DK, Light Worsted, #3)
    Stylecraft "Special DK": Grey, White, Citron & Lipstick

Dolphin Shirt (DK, Light Worsted, #3)
    Stylecraft "Special DK": Spring Green & Turquoise
    and
    Stylecraft "Special DK": Sherbet, Cream & Grey

V-Neck Shirt (DK, Light Worsted, #3)
    Stylecraft "Special DK": Silver, Graphite, Denim, Mustard & Black

Halter Top (DK, Light Worsted, #3)
    Stylecraft "Special DK": Aspen, Wisteria, Cream, Clementine & Pale Rose

Polo Shirt (DK, Light Worsted, #3)
    Stylecraft "Special DK": Walnut, Camel, Denim & Cream

Button-Front Shirt (DK, Light Worsted, #3)
    Stylecraft "Special DK": Copper & Gold

Shorts (DK, Light Worsted, #3)
    Stylecraft "Special DK": Spice

Jeans Shorts and Jeans Skirt (DK, Light Worsted, #3)
    Stylecraft "Special DK": Denim & Gold

Shortalls (DK, Light Worsted, #3)
    Stylecraft "Special DK": Sherbet & Cream

Beach Pants (DK, Light Worsted, #3)
    Stylecraft "Special DK": Grey & Citron

Pajamas (DK, Light Worsted, #3)
    Stylecraft "Special DK": Powder Pink, Parma Violet, Duck Egg & Spring Green

Underwear (DK, Light Worsted, #3)
    Stylecraft "Special DK": Grass Green

Cap (Worsted, #4)
    Red Heart "Super Saver": Country Blue
    Craft Smart "Value": Clay

Sun Hat (Worsted, #4)
    Craft Smart "Value": Light Pink
    Craft Smart "Value": Pink

Sandals (DK, Light Worsted, #3)
    Stylecraft "Special DK": Aspen

Beach Clogs (DK, Light Worsted, #3)
    Stylecraft "Special DK": Spice

Sneakers (DK, Light Worsted, #3)
    Stylecraft "Special DK": Wisteria & Cream

Snug Boots (DK, Light Worsted, #3)
    Stylecraft "Special DK": Gold & Camel

    (Bulky, #5)
    Bernat "Soft Boucle": Natural

Beach Play Mat (Worsted, #4)
    Loops & Threads "Impeccable": Clear Blue, White & Soft Taupe

Swim Ring (Worsted, #4)
    Loops & Threads "Impeccable": Cherry
    Craft Smart "Value": Light Coral

Beach Towel (Worsted, #4)
    Craft Smart "Value", Amethyst
    Loops & Threads "Impeccable": Petunia
    and
    Loops & Threads "Impeccable": Forest
    Craft Smart "Value": Sage

Raft (Worsted, #4)
>Loops & Threads "Impeccable": Eggplant, Fern, Pumpkin & Aqua

Bodyboard (Worsted, #4)
>Loops & Threads "Impeccable": Sunny Day

Beach Bucket (Worsted, #4)
>Loops & Threads "Impeccable": Cherry
>Lion Brand "Vanna's Choice": Kelly Green

Sand Shovel (Worsted, #4)
>Loops & Threads "Impeccable": Eggplant

Rainbow Beach Ball (Worsted, #4)
>Lion Brand "Vanna's Choice": Pink Grapefruit, Periwinkle, Aquamarine, Kelly Green, Terra-Cotta & Lemon

Mini FrizzBee (Worsted, #4)
>Loops & Threads "Impeccable": Citron

Sunscreen Lotion (DK, Light Worsted, #3)
>Stylecraft "Special DK": Aster, Spice & Turquoise

Clams (DK, Light Worsted, #3)
>Stylecraft "Special DK": Grey & Apricot

Sand Dollars (Worsted, #4)
>Craft Smart "Value": Mushroom

Sand Castle (Worsted, #4)
>Loops & Threads "Impeccable": Soft Taupe

Peanut Butter & Jelly Sandwich (Worsted, #4)
>Lion Brand "Vanna's Choice": Beige, Toffee, Gold & Cranberry

Tortilla Chips (DK, Light Worsted, #3)
>Stylecraft "Special DK": Saffron, Violet & Cloud Blue

Bottled Water (DK, Light Worsted, #3)
>Stylecraft "Special DK": Duck Egg & Green

Ice Cream Cone (Worsted, #4)
>Craft Smart "Value": Pink
>Loops & Threads "Impeccable": Soft Taupe

Orange Slice (DK, Light Worsted, #3)
>Stylecraft "Special DK": Spice & Cream

Paper Plate (DK, Light Worsted, #3)
>Loops & Threads "Impeccable": White

Beach Bag (Worsted, #4)
>Craft Smart "Value": Butter
>Craft Smart "Value": Light Gray

Ray the Stingray (Worsted, #4)
>Craft Smart "Value": Amethyst & White

Clawde the Crab (Worsted, #4)
>Lion Brand "Vanna's Choice": Chrysanthemum

Seabert the Seagull (Worsted, #4)
>Craft Smart "Value", White, Light Gray, Butter & Black

Starla the Starfish (Worsted, #4)
>Craft Smart "Value": Pink & Black

Sandy the Dog (Worsted, #4)
>Lion Brand "Vanna's Choice": Oatmeal, Barley, Black & Kelly Green

Tropical Fish Sleeping Bag (Worsted, #4)
>Red Heart "Super Saver Stripes": Retro
>and
>Red Heart "Super Saver Stripes": Parrot

Extras...just for fun!

Enjoy the
Beach Party Invitations
and
Coloring Page.

Other Books by Linda Wright

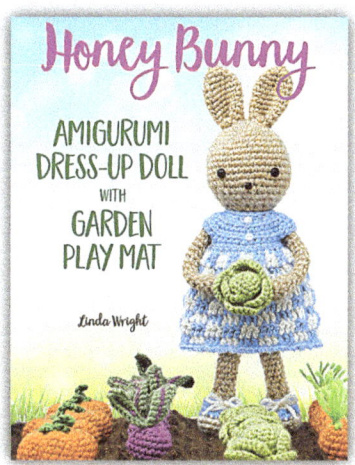

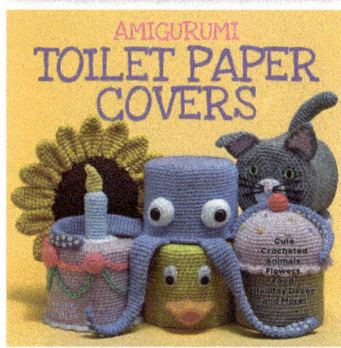
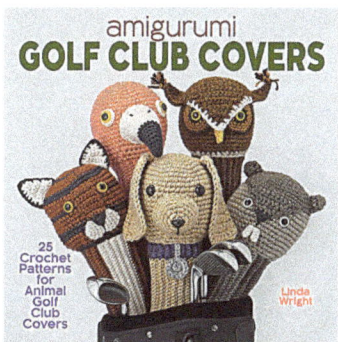

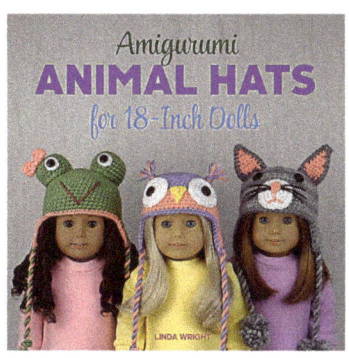
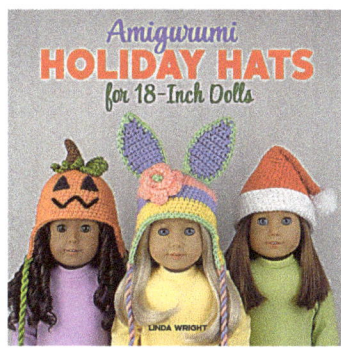

LINDA WRIGHT studied textiles, patternmaking and clothing design at the Pennsylvania State University and has had a lifelong love of creating. She is the author of various handicraft books including the groundbreaking *Toilet Paper Origami* and its companion book, *Toilet Paper Origami On a Roll*, as well as a collection of adult coloring books and numerous works of amigurumi-style crochet. To learn more about these fun-filled books, visit:

amazon.com/author/lindawright   **instagram.com/tporigami**   **pinterest.com/LindalooEnt**